SLOW COOKER CENTRAL

$UPER $AVER$

SLOW COOKER

CENTRAL

$UPER $AVER$

Paulene Christie

ABC Books

First published in Australia in 2017
by HarperCollins*Publishers* Australia Pty Limited
ABN 36 009 913 517
harpercollins.com.au

HarperCollins*Publishers*
Level 13, 201 Elizabeth Street, Sydney NSW 2000, Australia
Unit D1, 63 Apollo Drive, Rosedale Auckland 0632, New Zealand
A 53, Sector 57, Noida, UP, India
1 London Bridge Street, London, SE1 9GF, United Kingdom
2 Bloor Street East, 20th floor, Toronto, Ontario M4W 1A8, Canada
195 Broadway, New York NY 10007, USA

National Library of Australia Cataloguing-in-Publication entry:

Christie, Paulene, author.
Christie, Paulene, author.
Slow cooker central super savers / Paulene Christie.
ISBN 978 0 7333 3512 9 (paperback)
ISBN 978 1 4607 0655 8 (ebook)
Electric cooking, Slow.
Cookbooks
641.5884

Cover design by Hazel Lam, HarperCollins Design Studio
Cover images by shutterstock.com
Internal design by HarperCollins Design Studio
Author photograph by Tina Baills
Typeset in Adobe Jenson by Kirby Jones
Printed and bound in Australia by McPherson's Printing Group
The papers used by HarperCollins in the manufacture of this book are a natural, recyclable product made from wood grown in sustainable plantation forests. The fibre source and manufacturing processes meet recognized international environmental standards, and carry certification.

Dedicated to my husband Simon and our children
Caleb, Talyn and Ella
My everything
My forever and always
xx

Contents

INTRODUCTION

It doesn't seem so long ago that I was writing an introduction for the first Slow Cooker Central book – are we really here at book three already!?

I was a busy mum of three, a wife, a nurse; and as a result I was also very time-poor when I first discovered slow cooking. I wanted an easy way to get dinner on the table every night, something that was affordable and achievable. From that first night, dinner time was a breeze and I was hooked!

But I could never have imagined how drastically it would take over my life in just a few short years.

I initially created the Facebook group 'Slow Cooker Recipes 4 Families' in December 2012 as a place to gather the recipes I was trying. I hoped to inspire a few of my friends to share theirs too, and to build a little community of people who enjoy slow cooking. I could never have imagined what it would grow to become!

We are now the largest Facebook slow cooking group in the world! We have half a million members from all over the globe sharing our love of slow cooking and yet still we grow by hundreds every day.

In August 2014 we launched our website – www.slowcookercentral.com. To this day we continue to build our website, adding new recipes, blog articles and all manner of slow cooking tips, tricks, reviews and content. At the same time, we grow our group, share new recipes, inspire new people, make new friends and, in turn, are inspired by them.

Every day I feel so blessed to be a part of igniting a passion for slow cooking in so many people all over the world – to see people excited to try new dishes, excited to share their own creations and to have others try them too. Together we are expanding our skills, tastes and knowledge in all things slow cooking.

We are also real people. We are not fancy chefs in fancy kitchens, using exotic ingredients to cook fancy meals that most of us could never hope to replicate. We are real people, in real kitchens, cooking real food with real results.

Because everyone has different levels of skills, time and resources, we make sure we cater to all needs. This means some recipes are made completely from scratch, some are not. Some are focused on convenience and fast preparation, some are not. Some cost only a few dollars in total, some cost a bit more.

But no matter what the recipe, we always give you everything you need to deliver a delicious meal to your table – so you too can enjoy the success of slow cooking!

When ABC Books approached us to release the first Slow Cooker Central book it was a shock to say the least. I'd never even considered such an opportunity! What a fantastic way to share our passion with an even wider audience.

In 2015 *Slow Cooker Central* was launched and rocketed right to the top of the Australian bestseller list and stayed there for many weeks. In 2016 *Slow Cooker Central 2* did exactly the same thing! To this day the books continue to appear on bookshelves and in kitchens all over the world.

For book three we have decided to build on our first two books by focusing on an important aspect of slow cooking that everyone can relate to – saving money! No matter your own personal situation, everyone wants to save money. Slow cooking is a great way to do this on so many levels as you'll discover in this *Slow Cooker Central – Super Savers* edition.

Congratulations to everyone whose recipes feature in these pages. One of my favourite times of these past few years is the week the emails go out to those whose recipes have been selected for publication. The excitement and pride these people express is so contagious and thrilling! It's exciting to see your name in print for the first time or any time. If you are reading this, then you have it in print, in your hands right now – pretty exciting isn't it! :)

To everyone who is reading this book, to all our Facebook group members, to all of those who visit our website, and my amazing admin team who help me run the group – thank you for joining us once again on this amazing journey.

I feel like the luckiest lady in the world most days.

I began the group because I loved slow cooking.

I built the website because I wanted to deliver a better user experience.

I said yes to publishing our books because I wanted to share this joy with a wider audience.

I log on every single day of every year since because it's what I love doing.

I get to share my ideas, I get to share the ideas of others and I get to see those with no confidence in the kitchen discover the joys of slow cooking and blossom into confident chefs.

So thank YOU!

I hope you enjoy *Slow Cooker Central – Super Savers* as much as we have enjoyed compiling it for you. May you discover a host of new family favourites within.

Paulene Christie

SLOW COOKING ON A BUDGET

Money $ Money $ Money

It makes the world go round they say. We all want more of it, or at least, we want to make better use of the money we already have. If you are looking to save, slow cooking saves you money in so many ways! Let's look at how…

Save money on cooking costs

Slow cooking is certainly cheaper than running other appliances like ovens.

Of course there are many variables to consider including the size and model of your slow cooker and size and efficiency of your conventional oven, but overall the stats are well in favour of your slow cooker being the cheaper way to cook – even if it takes over eight hours instead of one hour!

Energy provider Ergon Energy advises that a slow cooker costs 4 cents per hour to run, while an oven costs 60 cents per hour.

So running your slow cooker for eight hours will cost 32 cents compared with 60 cents for just one hour of the oven (and that doesn't even account for oven pre-heating time).

More money in your pocket right there!

Save money on shopping costs at your butcher

Slow cooking saves you money at the butcher. The very nature of long slow cooking means your meat will still be lovely and tender. So you can buy a much cheaper cut of meat rather than top-shelf cuts. That's even more money in your pocket!

Cook in bulk and save!

A lot of slow cooker fans are cooking bigger meals and storing leftovers.

For instance, many people are using a large slow cooker with a six litre bowl to cook a soup. They fill it and store leftovers for another day.

The trend of using 'dump bags' for slow cooking is another easy way to save money. They're called dump bags because on the day of cooking you need only to 'dump' the defrosted bag contents into the slow cooker and dinner is done!

Often the longest process in slow cooking (even as short as it may be) is the preparation time – the dicing, peeling, measuring and prepping of your ingredients. Dump bags take the work out of this for you.

The basic technique is to prep all your recipe components in advance. Many people will do several batches of a single recipe, and often several recipes, on the one day. Each bag contains all the ingredients of a recipe already prepared. Make a note of any ingredient that you don't want to add in advance on the outside of the bag with a permanent marker and add it on the day when you cook.

Clearly label your dump bags and place them in the freezer. Pick the bag you want the day before you want to cook the recipe, pop it in the fridge to defrost, then hey presto, the next day you dump and run!

It makes sense to buy ingredients in bulk when using this method, which means smaller checkout charges – another great way to use your slow cooker to help your budget.

Save money on take-away and impulse buys!

Who hasn't got to the end of a long day and out of sheer exhaustion just decided to grab take-away for dinner instead of cooking a meal from scratch. We've all been there! Throw some tired, hungry kids into the mix and it's a recipe for disaster.

So save yourself and slow cook! Come dinner time, you'll have dinner all ready cooked, smelling amazing and just ready to serve. It's actually faster and easier than going out for take-away … and so much easier on the hip pocket!

If you work long hours, look for recipes that cook for eight hours or more to be sure your dinner is ready when you get home without being overdone.

Save money with smart choices!

Some recipes are going to be more budget-friendly than others based on their core ingredients. Choose wisely and you can immediately start saving money. For example, seafood and prime cuts of steak are rarely 'super savers', but recipes based on the following ingredients often are.

Chicken recipes: I cook more chicken than any other kind of meat. As you can see from our bursting chicken chapter in this book, lots of others like to do the same to save money. Look for cheap drumsticks or whole chickens on special. Even prepared fillets tend to be a lot cheaper than red meat! You can even use the raw bones for broth/stocks.

Sausage recipes: Cheap to buy, lots of flavour options and easy to use in a large bulky meal!

Mince recipes: So affordable and so so many options! Everything from Mexican to Italian and so much more!

Soup recipes: Six litres of flavour-packed soup goes a long way. Serve with crusty bread for even more serves! Soups are great to freeze for leftovers too.

Vegetable recipes: Cook as your main, or bulk out your meals with these affordable side dishes!

Use leftovers in a new meal!

For example, use a moist meat or a meat and veg meal from the night before to make a pie for the next night.

Use shredded meat in a new form on wraps, pizzas or tacos the next night.

Get creative – the sky is the limit on what you can create

Pick a recipe to match your budget

All the recipes in this book have been checked for approximate cost based on typical prices in Australian supermarkets and assigned to one of five $5 bands starting at under $5 (some of these recipes actually cost under $2) and topping out at between $20 and $25. Choose carefully in the shopping aisles and you can probably make these meals for less than we predict!

Aside from the side dishes and snacks, all recipes serve at least four people, while some will satisfy eight or more – great value!

So start slow cooking and SAVE MONEY easily right away!

RECIPES BY BUDGET

UNDER $15

UNDER $20

UNDER $25

SLOW COOKER HINTS & TIPS

We have here what we hope is a great collection of tips and tricks and frequently asked questions that we have gathered from the collective experience in our slow cooking community.

We've covered some really important safety do's and don'ts to help you to get the very best out of your slow cooking experiments while minimising the risks that other cooks may unknowingly take. The section on the tea-towel trick helps explain what that strategy is all about – you will see it mentioned a lot in our recipes. It helps us make many of the unique and unusual dishes we create in our slow cookers.

So BEFORE you start cooking, have a read through the hints and tips that follow – and then your hardest decision after that will only be deciding which great recipe from the book to cook first.

Can I use frozen meat in the slow cooker?

This is a hotly debated topic. The short answer is yes, you *could*, but no – you should not! Many people will tell you they have done so for years and it's never hurt them. However, that's probably more to do with luck than anything else. Don't follow dangerous advice. It's a risk that is quite frankly unnecessary, and we hope is one that you won't take with yourself or those being served your meals. Here's why…

Health concerns

Although some people will state that they cook frozen meat in their slow cookers, the health and food technology experts say that for food safety reasons you should bring your food to temperatures of 60°C (140°F) or more as quickly as possible. Some people assume that cooking frozen meat in a slow cooker works the same way as with other methods, but they are not the same. Food cooked in the oven or on a stovetop heats up much faster than in a slow cooker. Cooking frozen meat in a slow cooker significantly increases the amount of time it takes for food to reach the safe temperature target, and thus significantly increases the chances of you and your family getting food poisoning.

Cooker care

Cooking meat from frozen also increases the risk of a ceramic slow cooker bowl cracking as a result of the wide difference in temperature between the frozen food and the heating bowl. If the bowl cracks, your slow cooker is unusable.

On a similar note, you should always remove the food from your slow cooker dish before refrigerating it. The nature of the thick ceramic bowl means it retains heat and thus takes a lot longer to cool down to safe refrigeration temperatures, once again leaving your food too long in the danger zone.

In Summary

Please don't prioritise convenience over safety. It may be that you have to take the time to defrost your meat first, or you may in fact have to change the meal you had planned to cook for today until tomorrow when you can have the meat defrosted – but it's worth it. I for one will not take that risk with my loved ones. You are free to weigh up this risk for you and your family and hopefully make the safe decision for your home. Cook smart – cook safe.

How can I thicken slow-cooker recipes with a high liquid content?

Slow cooking can produce dishes with excess liquid due to condensation forming on the lid and the fact the lid stays closed so the liquid doesn't reduce as with some stovetop or oven methods. Here's a collection of tips and trick you can use to ensure a thickened consistency to your final dish.

Cornflour (cornstarch)

Mix 1–2 tablespoons of cornflour with 1–2 tablespoons of cool tap water and mix until it becomes a thin runny paste without any lumps (some people prefer to use rice flour or arrowroot flour). Pour this mix straight into your slow cooker dish 20–30 minutes before serving and stir briefly around whatever is in the pot. Then leave the dish to continue cooking, preferably on HIGH but LOW if the recipe requires.

This added cornflour will thicken the liquids in the recipe. If this amount of cornflour doesn't thicken the liquids sufficiently, you can repeat the process. But take care not to add too much cornflour to your recipe – one or two additions are usually all that's needed. Some people ladle the liquid out of the slow cooker into a saucepan on the stove and add the cornflour there. How you do it is totally up to you.

Gravy granules/powder

Substitute gravy granules for cornflour and follow the method as described above. The suitability of this option will depend on the recipe and whether the addition of gravy will suit it.

Grated potato

Grate 1–2 raw potatoes and add them to the slow cooker 30–45 minutes before serving. Stir them as much as you can around the solid ingredients. This will very quickly thicken the dish and the remaining cooking time will allow the potato to cook through.

Grated potato will only suit some recipes – those with vegetable or potato already in them or which would be complemented by the addition of potato.

You can use instant potato flakes in place of grated raw potato.

Lift the lid

Another option is to remove the lid of the slow cooker or at least place it ajar for the last 30 minutes of cooking to enable the sauce to thicken through evaporation. This is not ideal as the very nature of the slow cooker is to provide a sealed environment to maintain the cooking temperature – but it is an option.

Use less liquid to begin with

A natural consequence of slow cooking is the increased moisture content thanks to the drip condensation from the lid down into the food during cooking. Many people think meat has to be covered in liquid to slow cook it, but in fact it needs very little liquid. If you find a dish is regularly ending up with far too much liquid, reduce the liquid in the initial recipe next time you cook it.

The tea towel trick

While the tea towel trick (see the next page) is normally used when slow cooking cakes and breads, it can be used to absorb some of the condensation from the dish when following non-baking recipes. Please read important safety information in the section regarding the tea towel trick.

Flour toss

Tossing your meat in flour before cooking can also thicken the dish.

Pulling/shredding

Pulling or shredding your meat at the end of the cooking time (assuming this suits the dish) will also take up a lot of the excess liquids in the pot.

The tea towel (dish towel) trick

Quite a few of the recipes in this book, and many in the Desserts & Sweets chapter, will ask you to 'Cook with a tea towel (dish towel) under the lid'. The tea towel, which lies between the top of the slow cooker bowl and the lid of the slow cooker, acts to absorb condensation and stop it from dripping down into the food cooking inside. It's often used when you wouldn't want the cake or bread being cooked ending up soggy.

Note that this method has been devised by home slow cooker enthusiasts and is not recommended officially or declared a safe practice by slow cooker manufacturers. Please carefully read the following information before deciding for yourself if it's something you wish to do.

When using the tea towel trick, regular users suggest you fold up any excess fabric from the towel up onto the lid of the slow cooker, securing it to the lid handle, so it doesn't hang down over the hot outer casing of the slow cooker – this is very important for safety! A tea towel on the lid absorbs liquid during the cooking process, so it stays somewhat damp and is unlikely to burn.

If you have concerns about the fire hazards related to this practice, you can research the safety issues involved and inform yourself about the pros and cons. It is totally up to you to appraise the risks and decide whether it is safe to use the tea towel method with your slow cooker.

It is not recommended to use the tea towel in general slow cooking, but just as an optional measure to reduce liquid in a dish. If you decide to use this technique, do so only for cakes, breads and baking or recipes where water dripping is a major issue.

Please make your own decision regarding the safety of this practice. If in any doubt, do not do this. I personally recommend you don't leave your home when you are using a tea towel in this way, so that you are able to keep an eye on your slow cooker and the towel.

How can I remove oil and fat from a slow cooker dish?

There are several methods you can use to remove oil from your dish. First and foremost, you can reduce the amount of fat going into the dish at the beginning.

Be choosy

Choose lean cuts of meat, trim visible fat from meat and add little to no oil to your slow cooker recipes.

Prep it

Pre-browning or sealing meat in a frying pan is one way to remove some of the fat before cooking it in the slow cooker (read more about pre-browning and sealing meat on page 19).

Skim and discard

Perhaps the most obvious solution is to spoon that fat right out of there! Towards the end of the cooking process, the fat will often gather at the top of your dish so you can use a ladle or spoon to gently remove and discard it.

The ice-cube trick

Placing ice-cubes briefly on top of the dish will cause the fat to 'stick to' the ice-cubes (because the lower temperature causes the fat to solidify). You can then discard the ice-cubes and the oil right along with them.

The bread trick

Very briefly lay a piece of bread along the top of the dish. This will soak up the fat, which can be discarded with the bread or fed to a four-legged friend. But be very careful and always remove the bread with tongs, as it will be hot!

Some people use paper towel instead of bread to soak up the fats and oils, but if something is going to break down in my food, I would rather it were bread than paper.

Cool and skim

If you have the time or you are cooking a recipe in advance, you can cool the entire dish in the fridge overnight. The fat will solidify on top and you can remove it before reheating and serving the dish.

What does the AUTO function on my slow cooker do?

Many slow cookers have LOW, HIGH, KEEP WARM and AUTO settings. The AUTO function usually means the dish will begin cooking at HIGH for approximately 2 hours, then the slow cooker will switch itself down to the LOW temperature setting. (The dial itself doesn't move and will remain pointing to AUTO.)

This feature varies with different slow cooker models and brands, so always consult your user manual.

Are timers safe to use for slow cooking?

There is an important distinction between timers built in to a slow cooker and the wall kind that you plug into the power socket and then plug your slow cooker into.

A slow cooker with a timer function will generally switch your unit to a 'keep warm' mode after your pre-selected cooking time is complete. Most units will then only stay in this keep-warm mode for a limited number of hours for food safety reasons.

Wall timers are not recommended for slow cooking. For good reasons:

- Some people use them to delay the start time of cooking. This means the ingredients are sitting out, not cooking, for several hours before the slow cooker turns on. It's a recipe for a food-poisoning disaster.
- Some people use them to turn off the slow cooker at the end of the cooking time completely. This means your finished hot – and slowly getting cooler – dish is sitting out multiplying nasty bacteria in it until you get around to eating it. Again a recipe for a food-poisoning disaster. You would not cook a meal in your oven then just leave it in there or sitting on the kitchen bench for hours before eating it. A slow cooked meal is no different.

Definitely avoid timers designed for light fittings. These timers are not made to handle the load of a slow cooker. It could cause the slow cooker to burn out the element, or the timer itself could burn out or catch fire.

Cook smart, cook safe – please do not use wall timers for slow cooking.

Is it safe to leave my slow cooker unattended all day while I am out of the house?

In short, yes ... with precautions.

Slow cookers are designed to run all day unattended without posing a fire hazard. There are, however, further precautions you can take if you're concerned.

- I always place my slow cookers on top of my ceramic cooktop. This surface is designed to withstand high temperatures, after all. Just be sure never to accidentally have a hotplate turned on (I lost my first ever slow cooker to this happening when I melted its legs off!). If you don't have this option, placing the cooker on a glass-top trivet or heavy cutting board works in a similar way.
- Ensure flammable objects are not left touching or anywhere near the slow cooker.
- Move the slow cooker away from the wall and any curtains, etc.
- Do not use the tea towel method if you are out of the house.
- Always have a working smoke alarm and electrical safety switch in your home so that if you are home and the worst somehow happens, you and your family will be alerted to the danger and the electricity supply will shut off.

Is it okay to open the lid of my slow cooker to stir my dish or check on it?

Many of us have heard the tale that each time you open the lid of your slow cooker, it adds 30 minutes to the cooking time.

In practice, I have never personally found this to be true. If I am at home I am a habitual lid-lifter, often pausing to look at, stir, taste or even smell my dish throughout the day. And if anything, my dishes often cook much faster than I might expect.

However, slow cookers rely on the slow build-up of heat to cook food to perfection. Lifting the lid during cooking lets built-up heat escape and will lower the temperature in the slow cooker. Stirring the contents allows even more heat to escape from the lower layers of the food. Once the lid is replaced, it will take an amount of time for the food to heat back up to its previous temperature.

So the choice is up to you. Resist if you can, or don't. You will soon come to know your own slow cooker (or if you are like me and have several, you will get to know each of their little quirks and cooking times and temps).

Do I need to pre-brown, pre-cook or seal my meat before placing it in the slow cooker?

This is a debate that has no right or wrong answer. Some people are fierce advocates of browning meat prior to slow cooking it ... while just as many are fiercely against doing so.

At the end of the day it comes down to your own personal choice.

But let's look at the reasons on both sides of the debate so you can decide what YOU want to do.

Reasons to brown

- Faster cooking time – meat that is pre-browned won't need as much cooking time.
- Lock in moisture – sealing the surface of the meat can seal in extra moisture.
- Increased flavour – those caramelised, brown yummy bits on the surface of your meat that come with browning have lots of flavour that would otherwise be missing from your finished dish. Browning with herbs or spices can also increase the richness of these flavours in your recipe.
- Appearance – sometimes despite no change in taste, browned meat benefits the presentation of the final dish. By contrast, meat juices released from unsealed meat can sometimes mix with sauces etc making it appear as if cream-based sauces have split, when they have not.
- Fat removal – browning meat before cooking and then discarding the liquids produced is a great way to eliminate some of the fat from your finished dish. This is especially true when browning mince or ground beef.

- Thickening – meat dredged in flour, then browned before slow cooking, will add to the thickness of the sauce in the final dish.

Reasons not to brown

- Convenience – this would have to be the number one reason. Many of us are drawn to slow cooking by the sheer convenience of pouring a collection of ingredients into the bowl, turning on the machine and walking away. This convenience is lessened when you have to add extra steps to pre-brown.
- Time factor – pre-browning meat tends to reduce the cooking time for the recipe. This works against many slow cookers who rely on the extended slow cooking period to make it work for them, for example when they work all day.
- Less mess – while many new slow cookers allow the option to sear in the same bowl as you slow cook, this is not possible with the traditional ceramic bowl slow cookers. Thus browning a dish means dirtying a frying pan. Lets face it, who likes extra dishes? Not me!
- No option – we see many of our members using slow cookers when they don't have access to stoves/ovens. In this instance they do not have the option to brown their meats but shouldn't think that means they can't slow cook a dish that asks for it.

In summary

It really is up to you.

Personally I very rarely brown – maybe 5 per cent of the time that I slow cook, and then it's almost only those recipes which call for thin strips of meat to be flour coated and browned prior to slow cooking.

Some days and with some recipes you will want to – others you'll want to just dump in your ingredients, set and forget. Neither way is right or wrong, but hopefully in these pages we have given you the information to decide what's right for you.

Can I slow cook a whole chicken?

You sure can! And many people will tell you that having tried slow cooking chickens whole they will never do any other another way.

Here are some tips to keep in mind.

- You don't need to add any liquids to the slow cooker with your chicken. You will be really surprised by just how much liquid a whole chicken will release during cooking! And because a slow cooker is sealed, that liquid won't evaporate.
- Cook your chicken with the breast-side down. This keeps the breast meat sitting in the liquid that's produced during cooking so it won't dry out.
- If you are concerned there is too much liquid, or if you have a spice rub etc on your chicken that you don't want to get too immersed in liquid, you may choose to elevate the chicken above the bottom of your slow cooker by sitting it on some scrunched up aluminium foil balls, egg rings or even an inverted dish.
- When it comes to seasoning your chicken, your imagination is your only limit. Whatever spice, marinade or herbs you may use when you cook a chicken in the oven you can use just as well in your slow cooker.
- When your chicken is cooked it will be fall-apart tender! I like to get mine out in one piece by sliding two spatulas or large mixing spoons underneath both ends of the chicken and then quickly lifting it up and out onto a dish. An alternative method is to create a foil or baking-paper sling under your chicken prior to cooking. This can be used to grasp and lift chicken out at the end of cooking. This can be a large sling design or two strips crossed over to form a basket of sorts. Whatever works for you!

Help! I accidently cooked the absorbent pad from under my raw meat...

That awful moment when you first spot it... you have made a lovely slow cooker meal and you are just giving it a little stir before you serve it, when it appears: the absorbent pad from under your raw meat has accidentally ended up in your slow cooker – and *gasp* – you've cooked it!

Oh no!

What now?

Is your meal ruined?

Do you have to throw it out?

This actually happens a lot. More than you'd realise. At least a few times a week we see a member of our Facebook group looking for advice on what to do when they realise they've done this. So our goal was to get to the bottom of it and what it means for you and your pot full of otherwise yummy slow cooked food.

What are they?

Absorbent meat pads or absorbent meat soakers are the little packages that often sit between your raw meat and your butcher's tray. The purpose of the pad is to catch and absorb the liquid that naturally drains from raw meat and would otherwise pool in your meat tray and potentially spill out on you when it was tilted. It also helps prevent meat from sitting in a pool of raw meat juice that could breed bacteria and reduce shelf life.

The fact they are often black to begin with or soaked red with juices means that it's easier than you may think to tip your raw meat into your slow cooker from the tray without realising you have tipped in the pad as well.

What are they made of?

The butchers that I spoke to explained that the pads are usually made from paper pulp, plant fibres or non-toxic silicone with a plastic outer layer. They explained that they are approved for use in contact with food that is intended for human consumption, which means they have to be food-safe and non-toxic. They are not digestible, which means that even if you ate one it would go right through your digestive tract.

But what about when they are cooked? Does that change things?

Do I need to throw my meal in the bin?

The general consensus seems to be – if the pad is broken or pierced in any way, sadly yes, you should throw your meal out.

However, if the pad is intact you may decide to still eat your meal if you are comfortable doing so. A manufacturer of these pads (www.thermasorb.com.au) advises that if they are not broken then your meal is okay to eat. The poisons information hotline people agree. They report getting a lot of calls regarding this issue and advise that if the packet is broken your meal should be discarded just to be safe. However, in their experience, if the packet is intact most people will have no ill effects. From their experience, at worst those with a sensitive stomach may experience mild nausea or an unpleasant taste, but this is rare and most of their callers experience no ill effects.

So the choice is ultimately yours.

Help! My cream has split

In our slow cooking community we often see members posting their concern over split cream in their slow cooked dishes.

What is splitting?

A lot of people will refer to dairy products that have split as being 'curdled'. If your dairy product curdles during storage that's a problem and you should throw it out, don't use it. However, if it separates during cooking, it's more likely to be split and that is really only a change of appearance and texture. It's still perfectly fine to eat.

Why does it occur?

Sauces made with dairy products can split for several reasons.

- Low fat content – dairy products with high fat content are less likely to split.
- High heat – exposing dairy products to high heat, eg close to boiling, increases the likelihood of splitting.
- High acidity – adding dairy products to recipes with elevated acidic content can also cause splitting.

How can I prevent it?

- Choose higher-fat versions of your dairy product rather than the low fat varieties.
- If possible add the dairy product at the end of your cooking time rather than the beginning. You can even take it off the heat before you add it.
- When adding cream early, try whisking a teaspoon or so of cornflour into the cream first before adding it to your dish.
- Choose 'cooking cream' or 'creme fraiche' or double cream – these are less likely to split.
- Allow dairy products to come to room temperature before adding them. This can also help.
- Adding cream to a water-based recipe can cause splitting. Stirring regularly helps to avoid this.

What do I do once it's happened?

- Remember ... it's okay to eat. While a dish with split cream may not look perfect, it's certainly NOT a reason to throw it out!
- If the nature of the dish allows it, try giving the food a really good stir or whisk.
- Alternatively, try stirring through a little cornflour and water slurry.

Don't be discouraged! Next time just try the preventative measures. If all else fails, eat your meal with your eyes shut and you'll never know the difference *wink*.

Can I prepare a meal in advance and store it in the slow cooker bowl in my fridge overnight, then put it on the next morning?

Yes, you can if you wish. But it comes with risks!

Heating a cold bowl can lead to it cracking.

Also, the bowl and its contents will retain that cold for a long time and thus take even longer to reach safe temperatures once you begin cooking, placing you at increased risk of food poisoning.

A great way around this is to prepare the dish in advance but store it in the fridge in another large bowl, for example a mixing bowl. The food can then be poured into the slow cooker bowl in the morning. You still have all the convenience but without any of the risk.

What is the best way to clean my slow cooker bowl?

It happens to all of us sometimes! We finish cooking our recipe only to find a baked-on ring of cooked or burnt residue inside our slow cooker or on the base. Or maybe the inner casing of your slow cooker has stains in it? Don't despair – we've got the solution!

Basics

- The sooner you get it off the better!
- Avoid harsh abrasive chemicals or cleaning scourers.
- Always unplug the unit from the power source before cleaning.

Cleaning inside the cooking bowl

Most slow cooker bowls can simply be washed by hand in the sink. Some are okay for washing in the dishwasher. Be sure to check your manual for what is suitable for your model as not all models are dishwasher safe.

However, if you find yourself with a baked-on ring around the bowl that's hard to remove, the easiest way to get rid of it is remove the food, add water to a level above the baked-on ring and leave the slow cooker turned to LOW for a couple of hours. The ring should clean away much more easily then.

Some suggest placing a dishwasher tablet or even a denture cleaning tablet in the slow cooker while the water is heating in it for up to two hours but it is advisable to check with your user manual whether this is safe for your model.

Ceramic bowls and lids will not withstand sudden temperature changes. Do not fill the bowl with cold water when it is hot as it will crack.

Some ceramic bowls have a porous base and should not be left standing in water for extended periods because they might absorb water. It's fine to fill inside the bowl with water and leave it for any amount of time, but avoid leaving the entire bowl standing IN water.

Cleaning inside the main casing of the slow cooker

The metal housing of the slow cooker and electrical lead should NOT be placed in water! Be sure to completely unplug your unit from the power source and allow it to cool before any cleaning.

Over time you will find some of your food will splash down into the main casing of your slow cooker – under the cooking bowl.

It is important to ALWAYS CHECK YOUR INSTRUCTION MANUAL FIRST as to how your manufacturer recommends you clean your slow cooker.

Normally, electrical cables inside the base unit are fully sealed, but you should still exercise extreme caution in cleaning this main base unit – and again, never place the unit itself in water. If you can see heating elements inside the base do not clean or add water in this area and instead contact the manufacturer for advice.

For those who wish to proceed with cleaning inside the main casing, here are some suggestions I have gathered from members of the Slow Cooker Central community.

- Simply wipe the spill off with a soft, damp cloth and a small amount of dish detergent, especially if the spill is fresh or new.
- Clean using a mix of baking soda and vinegar on a cloth or sponge.
- Use a chalk-based cleaning paste like Gumption, which you can find in your supermarket cleaning aisle.
- Use baking soda and lemon juice. Combine and allow to foam then apply with a soft pad, sponge or scourer.
- While a soft green scrubbing type pad scourer should be okay, please think carefully before using a stronger steel wool type scourer as you could scratch your inner casing or bowl. A gentle sponge or rubber based scrubbing tool is ideal.
- Some report using a thin coat of oven cleaner (a fume-free version if you can), left for an hour or so then wiped off. If doing this I would recommend wiping over a few times with a damp cloth to minimise any smells next time you use the unit. Note: oven cleaners can be caustic and may even dissolve paint on the outside of your cooker, so use sparingly and cautiously.

Prevention is best

Rather than deal with the clean-up, try to prevent spills where you can!

- Spray your slow cooker bowl with some non-stick cooking spray before beginning.
- Line your slow cooker with baking paper for baked items or ones you think may stick.
- Use a slow-cooker liner bag or even an oven bag to slow-cook your dish.
- Follow the cooking time recommended in the recipe and avoid overcooking and burning.
- Do not overfill your slow cooker, which would increase the likelihood of spilling and staining in the casing area.

Are there any 'diet' recipes for slow cookers?

Almost every recipe can be adapted for weight loss or to make it healthier (with some obvious dessert-type exceptions).

Ways to adapt recipes to make them more waist-friendly include:

- Choose lean. Choose leaner cuts of meat than the recipe specifies. For example, go with low-fat mince, low-fat sausages or skinless chicken.
- Brown and bin. Brown meats before you slow cook them. This gives you an opportunity to drain and discard the fat rather than include it in your slow cooking recipe. Some people even like to boil their mince before cooking to remove fat.
- Trim the fat. Remove the fat before cooking, or remove fat or skin from the completed dish before serving.
- Bulk up. Add extra vegetables to your meal. If the dish you are cooking has few or no vegetables why not add some during cooking? Or when it comes to plating up your meal, load your plate with steamed or stir-fried veg to fill you up.
- Slash the salt. Choose low-sodium options for your ingredients. Even if the recipe doesn't specify it, I often change things like soy sauce or stocks to low-sodium options to cut the salt from the overall recipe.
- Choose low fat. In the same way that you can substitute low-salt ingredients, do the same with low-fat ones. Opt for low-fat yoghurts, milks and cheese, for example – pretty much anything that has a low-fat option.
- Selecting sides. What can make or break a meal when it comes to your waistline is sides. Choose wisely and your scales will thank you. Opt for healthier options like vegetables, salads and brown rice and the impact of the main meal is less.
- Portion power. Healthy eating is largely about moderation. You can enjoy that meal you really want, without having to totally overdo it. It's better to consume small portions of the foods that you crave rather than trying to resist them totally and ending up blowing out on a binge. Match the portion sizes of the various food groups on your plate with recommendations for a balanced and healthy diet.
- Love your leftovers. Why not cook extra when you do your next slow cooker meal? Then you can portion and store leftovers into healthy-sized meals all ready to take to work or to grab when the next attack of munchies strikes. It makes you less likely to make poor choices on impulse or opt for unhealthy take-away food.

- More of the same. As with all healthy eating plans, don't forget the basics. Drink plenty of water, eat mindfully, pack heaps of variety into your meal plans, choose fresh food when you can and move more!

Is it toxic to slow cook raw red kidney beans?

Yes, it is! But only raw beans. This does *not* include the canned varieties that are already cooked. A good explanation can be found at www.choosingvoluntarysimplicity.com:

'Raw kidney beans contain especially large amounts of [phytohaemagglutinin], and amazingly, eating just four or five raw or improperly cooked kidney beans can make a person extremely ill. Ingesting larger amounts can actually cause death. Other beans, including white kidney beans, broad beans and lima beans, contain the same toxin in smaller but still dangerous amounts.'

If you'd like to read further on this issue, these websites would be good starting points:

- www.choosingvoluntarysimplicity.com/crockpots-slow-cooking-dried-beans-phytohaemagglutinin/
- www.medic8.com/healthguide/food-poisoning/red-kidney-bean-toxins.html

Slow cooking cakes

Cooking cakes in slow cookers is out of the norm for a lot of traditionalist slow cooker users, so we wanted to include some advice on what can and can't be used in cake making in your slow cooker, and also to provide some general tips for getting the most out of your slow cooker cake making.

First and foremost, as detailed on page 15, the 'tea towel trick' is very important to prevent condensation dripping on your cakes when cooking them in the slow cooker.

Slow cookers can be used to cook packet (box) cake mixes as well as your own favourite from-scratch recipe.

But what do you cook the actual cake in?

There are three options.

1. Line your slow cooker inner bowl and cook your cake directly in it.

When doing this I find lining the bowl with non-stick baking paper not only prevents sticking but also gives you something to hold onto so you can lift the cake out at the end of the cooking time.

2. Cook your cake in a metal cake tin.

If you are concerned about using a metal cake tin dry in your slow cooker (ceramic bowls in particular are unsuitable for dry cooking) simply fill the bottom of the slow cooker bowl with 2–3 cm (1 in) of water first, then sit your cake tin gently in this water.

You can also elevate the cake tin off the bottom of the slow cooker to allow heat to circulate evenly around your cake. This can be achieved by resting the cake tin on a metal trivet, on metal egg rings or even on scrunched up balls of aluminium foil.

3. Cook your cake in a silicone cake tin.

Silicone cake tins (full size and cupcake size) are also safe to use in your slow cooker and will not melt. After all, they are intended for the high heat of conventional ovens.

When using non-ceramic slow cooker bowls I personally sit my silicone cake tins/cups directly onto the bottom of the slow cooker, without water, with no concerns. But if you prefer, you can elevate your tin using the methods described above. When using a ceramic cooker bowl I again add water first.

As with all non-traditional slow cooking, be sure to check your manual first and only do what you are comfortable doing.

Slow cooker fudge FAQs

Our members LOVE cooking fudge! We have hundreds of different varieties on the website, so you can browse for fudge online or use one of the recipes in this book. I've compiled some commonly asked questions about fudge to help you along the way.

What type of chocolate can I use?

Any type. Change the flavour of the chocolate to change the taste of the fudge. Milk chocolate, white chocolate, hazelnut chocolate, cookies and cream chocolate ... the options are unlimited. Some members use cooking chocolate, but others say the taste is not the same, so use your judgement. (Cooking chocolate does tend to melt at higher temperatures, so regular chocolate is ideal for the lower temp of the slow cooker.) If you are using chocolate that has a liquid-type filling, eg Caramello, you will need to increase the chocolate amount to account for this.

Can I add chocolate and lollies to my fudge

Yes. You can mix or top your fudge with anything you like. Make the base fudge, stir through whatever you like to add, then pour it into the lined tin to set. For example, you could add chopped nuts, biscuits, Mars bars, lollies (candies) ... whatever you like. Or pour your fudge into your tray to set then decorate the surface with these types of toppings. Again the options are endless.

How do I actually cook it? Do I need to stir it?

Break up the chocolate and place it in your slow cooker. Pour over condensed milk and add the butter and vanilla. LEAVE THE LID OFF your slow cooker and turn it on low and walk away. Every 10–15 minutes just pass by and give it a stir. It's that easy. As you near the end of the cooking time you may need to keep a closer eye on it but really it's just the odd stir along the way and there is nothing else to do.

Can I use any spoon to stir?

It's ideal to use a metal or silicone spoon when stirring your fudge. A wooden spoon can absorb some of the liquid from your fudge so it's best to avoid these. (Not to mention the fact that a metal spoon is a little nicer to lick clean!)

My fudge has seized – how can I fix it?

If things don't go to plan, your fudge might seize, which means it turns hard and weird instead of glossy. This problem can result from water getting into the fudge – remember, lids off for fudge to avoid condensation drips. Using a wooden spoon can do the same – remember, use a metal, plastic or silicone spoon for stirring fudge. There are a few approaches our members use to rescue seized fudge. Try stirring the living daylights out of it to bring it back to glossy. Others add a little splash of milk or condensed milk or even a bit more chocolate then stir like the clappers to bring it all back together. All is not lost. This is fixable – stir stir stir!

How do I know when it's done?

Everyone's slow cooker takes a different amount of time to cook. Simply melting the chocolate is not enough. After some time, you'll notice a very slight 'crust' on the surface as you stir, and the mixture will come away from the edges of the bowl slightly. This is the best sign that it's done. Some larger (hotter) machines may achieve this in half an hour. My 1.5 litre cooker that I use for fudge takes more like 90 minutes to achieve this. You will get to know yours.

What do I do with it once it's cooked?

Stir through any extras you want to add, then pour your fudge into a slice tray (I use one approximately 20cm x 20cm) lined with baking paper. You can use silicone moulds instead if you choose. Smooth the surface down to flat and add any decorations you like. If nothing is being added then simply place your tray in the fridge until set – approximately four hours should do it. Then use the baking paper to lift out your fudge from the tray. Remove the paper and cut the fudge quickly. Dipping your knife into hot water first can help cut cleanly.

How should I store my fudge?

Store your fudge in a sealed container in the fridge (make it a non-transparent container if you want to keep it from being rapidly gobbled up by the fudge fanatics in your home *wink*). The fudge will keep up to four weeks in a fridge. It can also be frozen for up to three months.

My fudge didn't set. What did I do wrong?

Please review the above tips. One of them will most likely reveal the reason your fudge did not set. You could also try returning your fudge to the slow cooker to reheat, adding more chocolate, then cooking it for longer. Not using enough chocolate is the number one cause of fudge not setting.

Pantry staples

One of the best ways to ease into trying new recipes is to have a supply of staple items in your pantry – on hand and at the ready for your next kitchen session. Build up your collection and all future recipes will be even friendlier on your budget.

Useful staples include:

- Baking powder
- Balsamic vinegar
- Canned or dried fruits
- Canned or dried vegetables
- Canned soups: condensed cream soups in various flavours (especially cream of mushroom and cream of chicken)
- Coconut cream and milk
- Cornflour
- Couscous
- Curry powder
- Dry packet soups such as French onion and chicken noodle
- Flour: plain (all-purpose) and self-raising
- Garlic: fresh or minced in jar
- Ginger: fresh or minced in jar
- Gravy powder/granules
- Herbs and spices: fresh in your garden, frozen in tubes or dried in jars and packets – as many as you can gather!
- Honey
- Lentils
- Mustard powder
- Parmesan: fresh or dried
- Pasta
- Pepper
- Powdered milk or UHT milk
- Rice
- Salt
- Sauces: sweet chilli, BBQ, tomato, worcestershire, soy, mint, oyster, hoisin
- Stock: powder, cubes or long life liquid (especially beef, chicken and vegetable)
- Sugar: brown and white
- Sweetened condensed milk
- Tinned tomatoes
- Tinned tuna
- Tomato paste
- Vinegar
- Wine: red and white
- Yeast

This is by no means an exhaustive list but it's a great start!

Goodbye, oven. Hello slow cooker! Converting oven and stovetop recipes for your slow cooker

Now you're hooked on slow cooking, I bet you'll find there are heaps of your family's favourite recipes that you have always cooked in the oven or on the stovetop that you want to convert for a slow cooker. And, for almost all of them, there is no reason you can't!

Here are some simple pointers:

- Reduce the amount of liquid. The condensation that forms in your slow cooker when in use means that recipes cooked in slow cookers need much less liquid then their traditional stovetop or oven counterparts. As a general rule try reducing the total liquid by approximately one quarter.
- Use cheaper cuts of meat. Remember that almost any cut of meat – even the cheapest and toughest – is sure to be tender after slow cooking. So feel free to replace more expensive cuts of meat with a cheaper option.
- Adjust the amounts of herbs and spices. Many people recommend reducing them by one half when converting a regular recipe for a slow cooker.
- Adjust the time. See the chart below to convert your stove and oven times to slow cooker times.
- Arrange the ingredients. When filling your slow cooker, put the root vegetables around the bottom and sides of your slow cooker, then place your meat on top.
- Take notes and experiment. It may take some trial and error to tweak your old favourites but it'll be worth it. Adjust liquids as you go (adding or removing) and keep an eye on cooking times. Take notes as you try new things so you'll always know just what worked the best for you. Soon you'll have a recipe you can use anywhere!

Stovetop & Oven Cooking Times	Slow Cooking on LOW Cooking Times	Slow Cooking on HIGH Cooking Times
15–30 mins	4–6 hours	1½–2½ hours
45 mins–1 hour	6½–8 hours	3–4 hours
1½–2½ hours	9–12 hours	4½–6 hours
3–5 hours	12½–18 hours	5–7 hours

SNACKS, SIDES & LIGHT MEALS

Jacket Potatoes

We love jacket potatoes – they are such a great way to use up leftovers and turn them into a brand new dish. Not to mention you can personalise each potato depending on each person's tastes. We often fill them with leftover bolognaise or pulled meats, or even just serve with a dollop of garlic butter and sour cream as a side dish.

Serves 4 as a side dish • Preparation 5 mins • Cook 4–4½ hours • Cooker capacity 5.5 litres

4 brushed (cleaned) potatoes
(I use potatoes slightly larger than a tennis ball)
Olive oil, to coat

1. Wash the potatoes, but leave the skin on. Pat dry then rub lightly with olive oil. Prick each potato with about 4–5 knife pricks.
2. Lightly oil 4 squares of foil. Wrap each potato in the foil. Place the potatoes on a small rack in the slow cooker, or elevate them on scrunched up pieces of foil or an upside down pie dish.
3. Pour about 2–3 cm (1 inch) of water into the bottom of the slow cooker.
4. Cover and cook on HIGH for 4–4½ hours or until the potatoes are tender – the timing will vary depending on your slow cooker. Check the water level and add a little more during cooking if needed.

Roslyn Potter

Savoury Wedges

This recipe for crispy potato wedges seasoned with chicken flavours and cheese is a winner in our home. I love the fact that it's a healthy way to serve a vegetable as a side dish or with meat or salad. I often serve it just with a simple salad.

Serves 6 as a side dish • Preparation 10 mins • Cook 5–6 hours • Cooker capacity 4 litres

6 large potatoes, cut into equal-size wedges
35 g (1 oz) packet cream of chicken soup mix
1 teaspoon garlic powder
1 teaspoon onion powder
1 tablespoon dried chives
1½ cups milk
½ cup white wine
1 cup grated tasty cheese

1. Toss the potatoes with the soup mix, garlic and onion powders and chives to coat.
2. Pour the milk and wine into the slow cooker. Add the wedges and turn to coat, adding 2–3 tablespoons of water if the mixture is too dry.
3. Sprinkle the cheese over the top.
4. Cover, putting a tea towel (dish towel) under the lid, and cook on LOW for 4½-5 hours or until potatoes are soft.
5. Uncover and cook on HIGH for 1 hour to reduce liquid and crisp up.

NOTE: Cooking time will depend on the size of potatoes used.

Laura Thomson

Sweet Potato Wedges

This recipe produces a moist, soft wedge, not dry as oven wedges can be, or oily as deep-fried wedges are. They are a great alternative to regular potato wedges and friendlier on the waist as a bonus. Serve with light sour cream and sweet chilli sauce.

Serves 4 as a side dish • Preparation 5 mins • Cook 1 hour • Cooker capacity 7 litres

1 large sweet potato
2 teaspoons olive oil
¼ teaspoon cracked black pepper
¼ teaspoon dried thyme
¼ teaspoon garlic powder
¼ teaspoon onion powder

1. Line the slow cooker with baking paper. Peel the sweet potato and cut into thick wedges.
2. Place the sweet potato into a large bowl, add all other ingredients and stir to coat well. Place into the slow cooker in a single layer.
3. Cover, putting a tea towel (dish towel) under the lid, and cook on HIGH for 1 hour, or until tender.

Paulene Christie

Sweet Potato Mash

Because I have multiple slow cookers, as many of you do, I love to slow cook my side dishes as well as my mains. It makes it so easy at dinner time then when all you need to do is serve from your slow cookers – no extra cooking required. This is a great way to cook your sweet potato and no chance of anything boiling over on the stove during those busy evening hours.

Serves 6 as a side dish • Preparation 5 mins • Cook 4 hours • Cooker capacity 5 litres

2 extra large sweet potatoes
1–2 tablespoons butter

1. Peel sweet potato and cut into chunks. Place into the slow cooker and cover with water.
2. Cover and cook on HIGH for 4 hours.
3. Drain the water and add butter. Mash until soft and creamy.

Paulene Christie

Cauliflower Mash

Cauliflower mash is a great low carb alternative to regular mashed potato. It's so easy to cook in your small slow cooker, ready to serve with your main meal. You can even build on this basic mash by adding a little garlic or shredded sharp cheese when mashing if you wish, but we mostly enjoy it just how it is.

Serves 4 as a side dish • Preparation 10 mins • Cook 2 hours • Cooker capacity 1.5 litres

500 g (1 lb 2 oz) roughly chopped cauliflower florets
1 tablespoon butter

1. Place the cauliflower florets into the slow cooker. Add 3 cups of warm water to cover the cauliflower.
2. Cover and cook on HIGH for 2 hours, or until fork tender.
3. Drain and transfer to large bowl. Add the butter and mash well.

NOTE: If cooking in a larger slow cooker, it may cook faster.

Paulene Christie

Slow-roasted Potato Slices

These potato slices are perfect as a side to any main. As an experiment this was a simple addition to add some carbs to my meal, but you could just enjoy them with salt and pepper for a hearty snack.

Serves 2 as a side dish • Preparation 5 mins • Cook 4–5 hours • Cooker capacity 7 litres

2 potatoes, washed
Spray oil, or olive oil for brushing
Pepper and chicken salt to serve, optional

1. Pre-heat the slow cooker on HIGH.
2. Cut the potatoes into thin slices, about 5 mm (¼ inch) thick. Spray or brush both sides with oil.
3. Place slices on a trivet in the slow cooker, not overlapping.
4. Cover, putting a tea towel (dish towel) under the lid, and cook on HIGH for 2 hours. Lift the lid occasionally to release moisture.
5. Replace tea towel with a dry one and cook for a further 2–3 hours, to your desired texture. Serve seasoned with pepper and chicken salt (if using).

NOTE: It is important to change the tea towel, so the slices aren't soggy.

Simon Christie

Quick Five Minute Scone

Arrived home late with hungry teenagers. Two ingredients and five minutes later we had a simple and easy dessert cooking away!

Makes 8 • Preparation 5 mins • Cook 1 hour • Cooker capacity 7 litres

200 g (7 oz) self-raising flour
200 ml (7 fl oz) cream

OPTIONAL FILLING SUGGESTIONS
Grated cheese, chocolate chips, chopped fruit, honey or jam

1. Mix the flour and cream together. Gather the dough and place onto a sheet of baking paper.
2. Shape into a rectangle about 1 cm (½ inch) thick. If using a filling, sprinkle or spread over the dough.
3. Fold in half to enclose filling, and using a sharp knife score the dough to make 8 scones.
4. Place in the slow cooker. Cover, with a tea towel (dish towel) under the lid, and cook on HIGH for 45 minutes–1 hour, until scones are cooked through.

NOTE: I used gluten-free flour and lactose-free cream. Depending on the type of flour used you may need a little extra cream.

Felicity Barnett

Chilli Jam

My daughter loves chilli, so after seeing a recipe that used chilli jam we decided to try making our own. Dairy, gluten, lactose and soy-free, this is easily adapted from mild to hot depending on how you like it.

Makes about 1 cup • Preparation 10 mins • Cook 4 hours • Cooker capacity 1.5 litres

3 long red chillies, deseeded and finely chopped (reserve seeds)
¼-1 teaspoon reserved chilli seeds (see note)
200 g (7 oz) Roma tomatoes, chopped
1 garlic clove, minced
1 eschalot, finely chopped
½ cup + 1 tablespoon brown sugar
1 tablespoon apple cider vinegar
1 tablespoon lemon juice

1. Place all the ingredients into the slow cooker.
2. Cover and cook on HIGH for 1½ hours. Tilt lid so it is slightly ajar, and cook for a further 2½ hours or until thick enough to coat the back of a spoon.

NOTE: For a mild jam use ¼ teaspoon chilli seeds, or for a hotter jam use 1 teaspoon seeds. If you really like heat, use them all! This will keep for up to 1 week in a tightly sealed container in the fridge.

Felicity Barnett and Susannah Durbidge

Cheesy Bacon Baguette

You could put cheese and bacon on just about anything and you'd sell it to me. I love both cheese and bacon, especially together. This fully loaded breadstick is great for entertaining or as a side dish at your next BBQ. People expecting you to unwrap a regular garlic bread from inside the foil will get a pleasant surprise at all the taste packed inside this baguette!

Makes 10 slices • Preparation 15 mins • Cook 1 hour • Cooker capacity 5 litres

30 cm (12 inch) baguette (French bread stick)
Butter, for spreading
100 g (3½ oz) diced bacon
1 cup grated tasty cheese
2 tablespoons mild American mustard
2 tablespoon chopped fresh chives

1. Cut the baguette into slices about 3cm (1 inch) wide, without slicing all the way through. Spread butter onto both sides of each slice.
2. Cook the bacon in a frying pan over medium-high heat until brown. Place into a large bowl and cool slightly. Add the remaining ingredients to the bacon and stir to combine.
3. Spoon mixture between slices of baguette. Wrap the whole thing in foil, folding to seal tightly. Place into the slow cooker.
4. Cover and cook on HIGH for about 1 hour or until the cheese has melted. Serve immediately.

NOTE: Prepare ahead of time and cook just in time to serve for great party food!

Paulene Christie

Lunch Box Pizza Muffins

This recipe is a great alternative to the regular sandwiches or tuckshop food at school. At just over $1 each they are much kinder on the wallet too. You can of course change the fillings to whatever you like best to suit all tastes. If taking them to my workplace or somewhere with a microwave I just remove the foil, place into a sheet of paper towel and heat for a minute to get the fillings back to piping hot.

Serves 4 • Preparation 10 mins • Cook 45 mins • Cooker capacity 7 litres

4 English muffins
4 tablespoons pizza sauce
80 g (2 ¾ oz) diced ham
1 cup grated tasty cheese
Optional toppings: pineapple, mushrooms, capsicum (pepper), chicken, onion or bacon

1. Split each muffin in half and lay cut side up on a square of foil. Spread each with pizza sauce then top one half of each with ham, cheese and any other topping. Close muffin and wrap up in foil. Place into the slow cooker.
2. Cover and cook on HIGH for 45 minutes.

NOTE: I cook my foil parcels directly on the bottom of my metallic slow cooker insert. If you are using a ceramic cooker, place the parcels on a trivet with about 1 cm (½ inch) water in the base of the cooker, ensuring it doesn't reach the level of your muffins.

Paulene Christie

Smoked Oyster Party Parcels

I went through an experimental phase of using puff pastry, and like all experimenters I had some fails and some wins. This recipe falls well and truly into the win category. Smoked oysters and cheese wrapped inside a puff pastry exterior – Yum! These are a perfect party appetiser.

Makes 16 • Preparation 15 mins • Cook 1 hour • Cooker capacity 7 litres

Spray oil
1 sheet frozen puff pastry
85 g (3 oz) smoked oysters, drained
16 small cubes colby cheese (or any cheese you prefer)
1 egg, lightly beaten

1. Spray the slow cooker with oil or line with baking paper.
2. Lay out the pastry and cut into 16 squares. Place an oyster and a small cube of cheese on each square. Fold up each parcel, seal and brush with egg.
3. Place the parcels, spaced apart, into the slow cooker.
4. Cover, putting a tea towel (dish towel) under the lid, and cook on HIGH for 1 hour.

NOTE: These would also be great with camembert or brie.

Simon Christie

Mini Kabana Dogs

Being a tradesman, I have often been to the bakery for pies, sausage rolls or whatever my eyes fall on for morning tea. Over the years I have enjoyed the odd sausage dog too. It's a sausage roll but instead of having a mince centre it's kabana wrapped up in the pastry. If you love these too, then look no further, my slow cooker enthusiasts! I have your recipe to make them right here and it's so simple!

Makes 4 • Preparation 10 mins • Cook 2 hours • Cooker capacity 5 litres

1 cheesy kabana (or smoked sausage of choice), ends trimmed
1 sheet frozen puff pastry
1 egg, lightly beaten

1. Line the slow cooker with baking paper. Cover and pre-heat on HIGH.
2. Cut the kabana into 4 equal portions. Cut the pastry into quarters and brush one end of each with egg.
3. Roll each piece of kabana in a piece of puff pastry, and fold ends to enclose. Brush pastry with egg.
4. Place into the slow cooker without touching the sides or each other.
5. Cover, putting a tea towel (dish towel) under the lid, and cook on HIGH for 2 hours.
6. Remove from slow cooker and stand for 5 minutes before serving.

Simon Christie

Fruity Overnight Oats

This cost effective, healthy and family-friendly breakfast is yummy hot or cold.

Serves 6 • Preparation 10 mins • Cook 6–8 hours • Cooker capacity 6 litres

2 cups rolled (porridge) oats
¼ cup shredded coconut
½ cup sultanas (golden raisins)
400 ml (13½ fl oz) can coconut milk
1 cup chopped fresh or frozen fruit
2 cups almond milk (or cow's milk)
1 tablespoon honey, if desired
Handful almonds, if desired
Good sprinkle of ground cinnamon and mixed spice

1. Place all the ingredients into the slow cooker with 1 cup water and stir to combine.
2. Cover and cook on LOW for 6–8 hours until oats are soft and creamy. Add a little more milk or water if you think it is necessary.

NOTE: If I'm at home I'll cook this on HIGH for 2 hours, just monitoring texture and adding more liquid if needed, but I prefer to cook on LOW overnight (timing with your slow cooker may vary). This recipe can be easily adapted using apple and cinnamon, pineapple and coconut, or blueberry and almonds.

Emma Dahm

Poached Eggs

I remember being asked by a member of our Facebook group one day if you could poach eggs in a slow cooker. I hadn't tried before then – but I like a slow cooker challenge – so I set about doing it to see if I could. It was so easy I now do it all the time! Without the precise timing needed when poaching eggs on the stove, I can instead set these to cook then go about my morning chores knowing that breakfast will be cooked for me when I return! It's also great if you are cooking for a large number of people, as you are able to poach as many as you can fit in all at one time so everyone can sit down to breakfast together.

Serves 2 • Preparation 5 mins • Cook 30 mins • Cooker capacity any size

Spray oil
4 eggs

1. Pour 1–2 cm (about ½ inch) of warm water into the slow cooker. Spray 4 silicon egg holders or cupcake cases lightly with oil – this helps the eggs slide out easy when cooked.
2. Crack an egg into each cup and place carefully into the water so as not to tip them over.
3. Cover, putting a tea towel (dish towel) under the lid, and cook on HIGH for 30 minutes or less – depending on how you like your eggs.

NOTE: This recipe can easily be adapted to cook more eggs (or just one) depending on your needs. It doesn't alter the cooking time dramatically.

Paulene Christie

Mushroom & Parmesan Eggs

I love breakfast eggs made in my slow cooker. It's great to be able to get on with my morning tasks knowing breakfast is taken care of for when I am done. I often serve mine with mushrooms which I love, so I decided why not combine the two right from the start. I often make a couple of extras to keep in the fridge for a healthy snack for the kids or myself later in the day.

Serves 2 • Preparation 5 mins • Cook 45 mins • Cooker capacity 5 litres

Spray oil
2 mushrooms, diced
2 teaspoons grated extra sharp parmesan cheese
4 eggs
Toast, to serve

1. Pour 1–2 cm (about ½ inch) of warm water into the slow cooker. Spray 4 silicon egg holders or cupcake cases, or even just cups, lightly with oil.
2. Add mushroom to each cup, and sprinkle with parmesan.
3. Crack an egg into each cup and season with salt and pepper. Place the cups carefully into the water so as not to tip them over.
4. Cover, putting a tea towel (dish towel) under the lid, and cook on HIGH for 45 minutes.
5. Serve with toast.

NOTE: These are also great served with avocado or baked beans.

Paulene Christie

Breakfast Slice

When I decided I wanted to make a breakfast recipe I knew it had to be with bacon – because I love bacon! I considered wrapping eggs in bacon but this was going to be difficult. My mum helped me to work out the next best way to do it ... an egg loaf with bacon top and bottom! Mum also helped me with the cutting of ingredients but I was able to do the rest myself with supervision. Now I ask for this most weekends for breakfast.

Serves 8 • Preparation 10 mins • Cook 1½ hours • Cooker capacity 6 litres

Spray oil
8 eggs
2½ tablespoons (50ml) thickened (whipping) cream
¼ red capsicum (pepper), finely diced
2 large rashers picnic bacon

1. Spray a silicon loaf pan lightly with oil. Whisk the eggs and cream, and stir in the capsicum. Season with salt and pepper.
2. Line the base of the pan with 1 rasher of bacon. Pour in the egg mixture.
3. Pour about 2.5 cm (1 inch) of water into the slow cooker. Lower the pan into the slow cooker.
4. Cover, putting a tea towel (dish towel) under the lid, and cook on HIGH for 1 hour.
5. Place the remaining bacon on top of the egg mixture (it should be set enough to hold it). Cook for a further 30 minutes or until cooked through.
6. Cut into slices to serve.

Talyn Christie

Chicken Potato Bake

This is a recipe I came up with one night because I wanted something that tasted a bit like chicken but in a potato bake. After going through the cupboards and fridge searching for ingredients that would taste nice together, I came up with the perfect solution. It's a creamy potato bake with a chicken twist to it and is perfect as a side dish to any meal. You could add any soup to change the flavour a bit, which makes this dish even better as you have a lot more options. It also cost next to nothing to make!

Serves 4–6 as a side dish • Preparation 10 mins • Cook 4 hours • Cooker capacity 3 litres

4 large potatoes, sliced
1 onion, diced
420 g (15 oz) can condensed cream of chicken soup
1 cup thickened (whipping) cream
1 chicken stock cube, crumbled
2 cups grated tasty cheese

1. Layer the potatoes in the slow cooker and spread the onion on top.
2. Combine the soup, cream and stock cube and pour over the potatoes and onion. Sprinkle with grated cheese.
3. Cover, putting a tea towel (dish towel) under the lid, and cook on HIGH for 4 hours.

NOTE: You can add diced bacon to the dish as well for extra flavour.

Kaylah James

Basic Tasty Leek & Potato Bake

This recipe is a family favourite, especially at a BBQ. We used to cook it in the microwave but I have found it develops a LOT more flavour if cooked in the slow cooker.

Serves 6–8 as a side dish • Preparation 10 mins • Cook 5–6 hours • Cooker capacity 5 litres

300 ml (10 fl oz) thickened (whipping) cream
300 g (10½ oz) sour cream
24 g (¾ oz) sachet leek and potato soup mix
6 small to medium potatoes, diced or sliced
1 garlic clove, minced
3 rashers bacon, chopped
1 small to medium onion, diced

1. Place the cream, sour cream and soup mix in a bowl and mix until well combined.
2. Put the remaining ingredients into the slow cooker, add the cream mixture and stir to combine.
3. Cover and cook on HIGH for 2 hours, then reduce to LOW and cook for 3–4 hours.

NOTE: If you have an AUTO setting, use that to cook for 5–6 hours. If you wish you can add grated cheese to the top once cooked, and let it continue cooking for an extra 30 minutes. You can pre-cook the bacon and onion for extra flavour if you like but it's not a must.

Bea Arnel

Cheesy Broccoli & Cauliflower Bake

There is something so yummy about broccoli and cauliflower covered with a lovely cheesy sauce. It's old style comfort food, great to serve at a BBQ or as a side dish to your regular dinner main. I cook this one directly in the serving dish so that I then can deliver it straight to the table. If you prefer you can do this with just broccoli or just cauliflower instead of the combination.

Serves 5 as a side dish • Preparation 15 mins • Cook 1 hour 45 mins • Cooker capacity 7 litre (or whatever fits your dish)

500 g (1 lb 2 oz) bag of mixed broccoli and cauliflower pieces (or fresh cut yourself if you prefer)
200 ml (7 fl oz) cooking cream
1 cup grated tasty cheese
1 cup grated mozzarella cheese

1. Pour about 2.5 cm (1 inch) warm water into the slow cooker – but ensure the water level is not high enough that it could flow into your cooking dish when it is placed in the water bath to cook.
2. Place the broccoli and cauliflower into a heatproof dish. Mix the cream with the tasty cheese and pour over the vegetables.
3. Carefully lower the dish into the water bath in your slow cooker.
4. Cover, putting a tea towel (dish towel) under the lid, and cook on HIGH for 1½ hours or until the vegetables are fork tender.
5. Scatter the mozzarella cheese over the vegetables and cook for another 15 minutes or until the mozzarella has melted.
6. Lift the cooking dish carefully out of the slow cooker bowl.

Paulene Christie

Chicken & Bacon Paté

One of my friends was telling me how simple it was to make paté, so I thought I'd give it a go! I switched out cream for the cream of chicken soup to add extra flavour.

Makes about 3 cups • Preparation 20 mins • Cook 3 hours • Cooker capacity 3 litres

500 g (1 lb 2 oz) chicken livers, chopped
250 g (9 oz) bacon, chopped
1 onion, diced
2 garlic cloves, minced
1 cup chicken stock
420 g (15 oz) can condensed cream of chicken soup

1. Fry the chicken livers, bacon, onion and garlic in a large non-stick frying pan over medium-high heat until browned.
2. Add the chicken stock and bring just to the boil. Transfer the mixture to the slow cooker and stir in the soup. Season with salt and pepper.
3. Cover and cook on HIGH for 3 hours.
4. Cool, then blend or process until smooth. Transfer to a bowl and smooth the surface. Cover and refrigerate until set.

NOTE: You could use cream of mushroom soup and add mushrooms for a different flavour if you like.

Kelly Brereton

Cheesy Bacon Scrolls with Green Tomato Relish

I admit it – I LOVE green tomato relish. It was only natural that I came up with a scroll variety that included this. I've always enjoyed it with ham and bacon in the past so the combination with a cheesy scroll was fantastic. I'm quite new to making my own dough, but this couldn't have been easier. You could always add extra toppings if you like.

Makes 14 • Preparation 15 mins • Cook 1½ hours • Cooker capacity 7 litres

2 cups self-raising flour
1 cup Greek yoghurt
½ cup green tomato relish
150 g (5½ oz) diced bacon
1 cup grated tasty cheese

1. Combine the flour and yoghurt and mix to a soft dough. Turn out onto a floured surface and knead briefly, then roll out to a flat square 1–1.5 cm (about ½ inch) thick.
2. Spread with relish. Sprinkle with the bacon, then ⅔ of the grated cheese.
3. Roll up into a log shape then use a sharp knife to cut into slices around 2 cm (¾ inch) thick.
4. Line the slow cooker with baking paper, and lay the slices flat onto the paper. Sprinkle the remaining cheese over the scrolls.
5. Cover, putting a tea towel (dish towel) under the lid, and cook on HIGH for 1½ hours.

Paulene Christie

Cheese & Salami Sticks

These are a great addition to a party table or snack platter. I used cheese sticks for convenience but you could slice your own sticks of cheese off the block if you prefer. Change the salami heat to easily change the overall heat of the final dish too. Remember to use the tea towel in this one to ensure the pastry stays dry during cooking.

Makes 8 sticks • Preparation 10 mins • Cook 1½ hours • Cooker capacity 7 litres

2 sheets frozen puff pastry
8 slices shaved mild salami
8 cheese sticks
1 egg, lightly beaten
Spray oil

1. Lay out the sheets of puff pastry on a bench and use a sharp knife to cut into quarters (no need to separate the quarters at this stage).
2. On each quarter lay one slice of salami and one cheese stick, placing them at the top of the square. Roll up the pastry to enclose the salami and cheese. Pinch both ends of the pastry to seal. Pierce twice along the top of each parcel with a fork, then brush with egg.
3. Spray the slow cooker bowl lightly with oil and place the sticks into the slow cooker.
4. Cover, putting a tea towel (dish towel) under the lid, and cook on HIGH for 1 hour 15 minutes. Turn over and cook for a further 15 minutes.

NOTE: Enjoy these hot, but take care as the filling will be really hot!

Paulene Christie

Fully Loaded Impossible Quiche

I needed a budget friendly recipe that would use all the bits and pieces of foods I had in the fridge at the end of the week and I had plenty of eggs so it needed to be egg-based. I didn't really want to spend time making a crust. I knew there was such a thing as an impossible pie so I searched the internet to get the main technique then set about making my own.

Serves 6 • Preparation 20 mins • Cook 4½ hours • Cooker capacity 4 litres

1 small onion, diced
1 small tomato, diced
5 mushrooms, sliced
5 rashers bacon, chopped
½ x 420 g (15 oz) can corn kernels, drained, ¾ cup liquid reserved
1 cup grated tasty cheese
12 pitted black or green olives, halved
12 pickled jalapeno slices (optional)
½ cup plain atta flour (see note)
1 tablespoon each chopped fresh oregano, thyme and parsley (or 1 teaspoon each dried)
4 eggs
300 ml (10 fl oz) light evaporated milk

1. Place the onion, tomato, mushrooms, bacon, corn, cheese, olives, jalapenos (if using), flour and herbs in a large bowl. Stir gently until combined.
2. Grease the slow cooker and line with baking paper. Spread the mixture into the slow cooker.
3. Whisk the eggs, evaporated milk and reserved corn liquid until smooth. Pour over the filling.
4. Cover, putting a tea towel (dish towel) under the lid, and cook on LOW for 4½ hours or until set but still slightly wobbly (it will continue cooking as it cools).
5. Turn off cooker and leave until the quiche is cool enough to handle and has become firm (if it is too warm it may collapse). Invert carefully onto a plate. Some liquid will seep out from the mushrooms – this is normal.

NOTE: Atta flour is a fine wholemeal flour from India. You can use white or regular wholemeal flour if you like. My slow cooker is about 20 cm (8 inch) diameter round. If you use a larger size you may need to increase the ingredients accordingly or you could end up with a giant omelette! Alternatively pour the mixture into a round greased and lined cake tin and place on egg rings inside a large slow cooker. Pour in enough water to come up to the base of the pan.

Keryn Wolff

Mac & Cheese

This recipe is great for lunches, kids' meals, freezer meals or even as a side. I wanted to create one like I grew up eating – Kraft boxed Mac & Cheese. This is as close as I could get to my childhood favourite.

Serves 4–6 • Preparation 10 mins • Cook 2 hours • Cooker capacity 5 litres

150 g (5½ oz) butter, chopped
4 cups milk
¼ teaspoon beef stock paste
500 g (1 lb 2 oz) Kraft Cheddar (from the shelf, not chilled), cubed
500 g (1 lb 2 oz) macaroni

1. Place the butter into the slow cooker and add the milk, stock paste and 4 cups hot water.
2. Add the cheese and pasta and stir to combine.
3. Cook, uncovered, on HIGH for 2 hours, stirring occasionally.
4. Season with salt and pepper to taste.

NOTE: Don't be afraid to add more ingredients. You could sneak in some veggies or add everyone's favourite – bacon!

Danette Pendleton

Roast Vegetables

For this recipe I use a searing (metallic bowl) slow cooker with a large base surface area. I spread the vegetables out into a single layer and don't need to turn them during cooking, but if you wanted to I would do so very gently so as not to break them apart. Use whatever vegetables you prefer for your family.

Serves 5 as a side dish • Preparation 10 mins • Cook 3 hours • Cooker capacity 7 litres

Vegetables such as potato, sweet potato, pumpkin, carrot and onion
1 tablespoon olive oil
¼ teaspoon garlic powder
½ teaspoon dried rosemary

1. Cut the vegetables into large chunks (for example, I cut medium potatoes into quarters).
2. Place vegetables and the remaining ingredients into a bowl or bag and season with cracked black pepper. Toss to coat.
3. Transfer the vegetables to the slow cooker bowl in a single layer.
4. Cover and cook on HIGH for 3 hours or until tender.

Paulene Christie

Super Simple Quick Quiche

This is so simple to make! Served with a side salad it's a fantastic summer budget meal the whole family can enjoy. It also makes a great addition to lunchboxes for your little ones or an easy breakfast to grab on the run as you race out the door. You could substitute ham for the bacon if you prefer.

Serves 4 • Preparation 10 mins • Cook 1 hour • Cooker capacity 6 litres

8 eggs
100 ml (3½ fl oz) cooking cream
200 g (7 oz) diced bacon
½ cup sliced spring onions (scallions)

1. Whisk the eggs and cream together, then add the bacon and onions and season with salt and pepper.
2. Line the slow cooker with baking paper. Gently pour the mixture into the slow cooker.
3. Cover, putting a tea towel (dish towel) under the lid, and cook on HIGH for 1 hour.
4. Cut into slices to serve.

Paulene Christie

Easy Pizza Supreme

Have you ever thought of pizza in a slow cooker? Neither had I, but I like a slow cooker challenge. The result is this awesome better-than-a-bought-one pizza! Excellence in every slice. I hope if you try this you will be as impressed as I was. You can mix and match any toppings you like, half and half or plain triple cheese. Your imagination is your only limit.

Makes 1 family pizza (8 slices) • Preparation 15 mins + 20 mins resting • Cook 2 hours • Cooker capacity 7 litres

285 g (10 oz) packet pizza base mix
Pizza sauce, to taste
150 g (5½ oz) sliced chorizo
100 g (3½ oz) sliced bacon
100 g (3½ oz) drained pineapple pieces
1 tomato, sliced
2 mushrooms, sliced
5 olives, sliced
50 g (1¾ oz) ham, diced
1 cup grated mozzarella cheese
BBQ sauce, to serve (optional)

1. Prepare pizza dough according to packet directions. Knead dough and rest for 20 minutes. Ten minutes before end of resting time preheat your slow cooker on HIGH. If your cooker manual recommends against preheating, add 10 minutes to the total cooking time.
2. Press or roll out dough and place into the slow cooker, making sure it goes all the way to the edges. Cook on HIGH with lid off for 1 hour.
3. Spread pizza sauce onto the pizza base in the cooker, and add the toppings.
4. Cover, putting a tea towel (dish towel) under the lid, and cook on HIGH for 1 hour.
5. Serve drizzled with BBQ sauce (if using).

Simon Christie

Creamy Potato Bake with Chorizo & Bacon

I love a good potato bake! It's such a great side dish to a BBQ or any number of main meals. Think of this as the loaded potato bake of your dreams – the chorizo and bacon give it so much flavour and that creamy cheesy sauce surrounding it is to die for! If your budget is a little tight you can replace the chorizo with more bacon, but personally I find it a worthwhile expense for the taste it delivers.

Serves 6 as a side dish • Preparation 15 mins • Cook 4½ hours • Cooker capacity 5 litres

Spray oil
850 g (1 lb 14 oz) small washed potatoes, skin on
1 small brown onion, thinly sliced
100 g (3½ oz) diced bacon
100 g (3½ oz) chorizo sausage, diced
2 teaspoons minced garlic
½ teaspoon cracked black pepper
2 cups cooking cream
1½ cups grated tasty cheese
Sprinkle of paprika

1. Spray the slow cooker bowl lightly with oil. Re-wash the potatoes to ensure they are nice and clean, then slice them thinly – if you cut them thick you will need to increase the cooking time to ensure they are tender.
2. Lay half the sliced potatoes into the slow cooker. Add the onion, bacon and chorizo. Cover with the remaining potatoes.
3. Add the garlic and pepper to the cream and mix well. Pour over the potatoes.
4. Cover, putting a tea towel (dish towel) under the lid, and cook on HIGH for 2 hours then reduce to LOW and cook for 2 hours.
5. Scatter the cheese over the potato and sprinkle with paprika. Replace the lid and tea towel and cook for a further 30 minutes, so the cheese can melt. Serve straight from slow cooker.

NOTE: Cooking cream is less likely to split during cooking than regular cream. If you have the AUTO function, use that and cook for 4½ hours. I use the paprika on top as it gives the look of browning – but you can finish it in the oven if you prefer.

Paulene Christie

Zucchini Slice

This is a delicious family recipe I wish to share with you all. My kids absolutely love this. It was passed down by my mum to me, so we are going to keep the tradition going. I don't usually like capsicum but in this recipe I can't get enough.

Serves 4–6 • Preparation 20 mins • Cook 3–4 hours • Cooker capacity 6 litres

Spray oil
1 zucchini, coarsely grated
1 large brown onion, finely chopped
1 cup grated tasty cheese
6 eggs, lightly beaten
250 g (7 oz) diced bacon
1 green capsicum (pepper), chopped
1 red capsicum (pepper), chopped
1 cup self-raising flour

1. Line the slow cooker with baking paper and spray with cooking oil.
2. Place all the ingredients except the flour into a mixing bowl and mix until combined.
3. Add the flour a little at a time, mixing until combined after each addition. Pour into the slow cooker.
4. Cover and cook on HIGH for 3–4 hours, until set.

NOTE: This is yummy served hot or cold, and is lovely with a salad.

Trinity Simmons

Zucchini & Choko Slice

I needed to use up a few things in the fridge so I made this. It's great served hot or cold (for the summer heat!) with salad and garlic bread. It's easy to make and seems to be enjoyed by even the fussiest of eaters!

Serves 8 • Preparation 20 mins • Cook 2–3 hours • Cooker capacity 6 litres

9 eggs
⅔ cup milk
2 zucchini, coarsely grated
2 chokos, coarsely grated
1 sweet potato, coarsely grated
1 carrot, coarsely grated
1 onion, finely chopped
4 rashers bacon, chopped
1 cup shredded tasty cheese
1⅓ cups self-raising flour

1. Line the slow cooker with baking paper. Whisk the eggs and milk together, and combine with the remaining ingredients. Season with salt and pepper. Pour into the slow cooker.
2. Cover, with a tea towel under the lid, and cook on HIGH for 3 hours, until set.

NOTE: This is a very versatile recipe, as you can substitute other vegetables if you don't have these on hand.

Melissa Walton

SOUP

Easy Peasy Broccoli Soup

I make this healthy soup in the winter for two reasons: 1. Who doesn't love soup on a cold evening? 2. Broccoli is super cheap in the winter which means I can feed my family a healthy dinner for about $5!

Serves 6 • Preparation 5 mins • Cook 3 or 6 hours • Cooker capacity 6 litres

1 kg (2 lb 3 oz) broccoli, chopped (including stalks)
½ onion, diced
1 teaspoon minced garlic
2 salt-reduced stock cubes, crumbled (vegetable or chicken)
Cream or sour cream, chilli flakes and crusty bread, to serve

1. Combine all the ingredients and 6 cups water in the slow cooker.
2. Cook on HIGH for 3 hours or LOW for 6 hours.
3. Use a stick blender to blend until smooth (take care as it will be hot).
4. Serve in big bowls with a dollop of cream or sour cream, a sprinkle of chilli flakes and crusty bread on the side.

Fiona Masters

Pumpkin Soup

This is super simple and super tasty! There's no need to pre-cook anything, and it freezes really well.

Serves 8–10 • Preparation 20 mins • Cook 6 hours • Cooker capacity 6 litres

1.5 kg (3 lb 5 oz) Kent (Jap) pumpkin, chopped
4 cups chicken stock
250 g (9 oz) potatoes, chopped
250 g (9 oz) sweet potato, chopped
250 g (9 oz) brown onion, chopped
1 tablespoon minced garlic
1–2 tablespoons curry powder (see note)
¼ teaspoon salt
Sour cream, to serve

1. Combine all the ingredients (except sour cream) in the slow cooker.
2. Cover and cook on LOW for 6 hours.
3. Use a stick blender to blend until smooth (take care as it will be hot). Serve topped with a small dollop of sour cream.

NOTE: We like a curry bite so we use 2 tablespoons curry powder, but you can reduce to as little as 1 teaspoon depending on your taste.

Sharon King

Creamy Potato, Leek & Bacon Soup

This is a delicious and wholesome meal, thoroughly enjoyed by all ages.

Serves 4 • Prep time 15 mins • Cook time 5 hours • Capacity 3.5 litres

1 kg (2 lb 3 oz) potatoes, diced
4 cups vegetable stock
2 leeks, sliced
5 rashers bacon, chopped
3 teaspoons minced garlic
½ cup cream

1. Combine all the ingredients (except the cream) in the slow cooker.
2. Cover and cook on LOW for 5 hours.
3. Use a stick blender to blend until smooth (take care as it will be hot). Stir through cream and serve.

Jenny Krahe

Tomato, Bacon, Basil & Chilli Soup

I came up with this recipe one day when I was making just a simple tomato soup. Tomato soup is great but I wanted to spice it up a bit...so why not add bacon, basil and chilli? It worked a treat. You can add more or less chilli, depending on your taste.

Serves 2 • Preparation 10 mins • Cook 6 hours • Cooker capacity 3 litres

2 x 400 g (14 oz) cans diced tomatoes
5 bacon rashers, chopped
½ cup vegetable stock
2 tablespoons minced garlic
1 tablespoon sweet chilli sauce
2 teaspoons finely chopped chilli
10–15 fresh basil leaves, plus extra to serve
Crusty bread, to serve

1. Combine all the ingredients in the slow cooker.
2. Cover and cook on LOW for 6 hours.
3. Use a stick blender to blend until smooth (take care as it will be hot). Serve topped with extra basil leaves, with crusty bread.

NOTE: You may like to brown the bacon before putting it into the slow cooker.

Tara Beynon

Minestrone Soup

I love how easy this recipe is. I normally have most of the ingredients in the cupboard so it makes it a cheap meal as well.

Serves 4–6 • Preparation 15 mins • Cook 4 or 8 hours • Cooker capacity 6 litres

800 g (1 lb 12 oz) can diced tomatoes
3 cups beef stock
1 onion, finely diced
2 garlic cloves, minced
4 rashers bacon, chopped
2 carrots, diced
2 celery stalks, diced
Sprinkle of mixed herbs
2–3 bay leaves
100 g (3½ oz) macaroni
400 g (14 oz) can cannellini beans, rinsed and drained
100 g (3½ oz) green beans
Grated parmesan cheese and crusty bread, to serve

1. Combine the tomatoes, stock, onion, garlic, bacon, carrot, celery, mixed herbs and bay leaves in the slow cooker.
2. Cook on LOW for 7½ hours or HIGH for 3½ hours.
3. Put the macaroni into a heatproof bowl with and cover with boiling water. Stand for 10 minutes.
4. Drain the macaroni and place into the slow cooker with the cannellini beans and green beans. Stir to combine and cook for 30 minutes or until the macaroni is cooked.
5. Season with salt and pepper to taste, and serve with parmesan and crusty bread.

Cheree Bone

Nana's Meat & Vegie Soup

This soup was made by my Nana all the time. I learnt it from my mum and now I make it all the time. It's awesome for a cold winter's day, full of veggies with the flavours of meat as well.

Serves 8 • Preparation 15 mins • Cook 7–8 hours • Capacity 5 litres

4–6 lamb neck chops (you can use beef soup bones but lamb is better)
2–3 carrots, grated
2–3 potatoes, grated
2 onions, finely chopped
1 cup pearl barley
1 teaspoon minced garlic
4 beef stock cubes

1. Place the chops into the slow cooker. Add the carrots, potatoes, onions, pearl barley and garlic on top.
2. Crumble the stock cubes and dissolve in 1 cup of boiling water. Pour into the slow cooker. Season with salt and pepper, and add 12 cups water.
3. Cover and cook on LOW for 5 hours.
4. Take the lamb from the slow cooker, and shred the meat from the bones. Return the meat to the slow cooker and discard the bones. Cook on LOW for a further 2–3 hours.

Hannah Turley

Manly Cauli Soup

This soup is creamy and hearty, and leaves everyone feeling full. It has 'bacony' goodness but is still lean. It's also great for an entree if you are trying to cut main meal sizes and budgets!

Serves 8 • Preparation 10 mins • Cook 5 hours • Cooker capacity 6–8 litres

1 cauliflower, chopped
1 leek, white part only, chopped
2 teaspoons minced garlic
4 rashers bacon, trimmed of fat, finely chopped
4 cups chicken stock
½ cup shaved parmesan cheese
250 ml (9 fl oz) thin (pouring) cream (see note)
Fresh bread rolls or sourdough bread, to serve

1. Place the cauliflower, leek, garlic, bacon and stock in the slow cooker.
2. Cover and cook on HIGH for 1 hour, then reduce to LOW and cook for about 4 hours or until the cauliflower is soft.
3. Use a stick blender to blend until smooth (take care as it will be hot). Add the parmesan and stir until melted, then stir in the cream.
4. Serve with fresh bread rolls or sourdough bread.

NOTE: To make this even cheaper, replace the leek with an onion and the Parmesan with grated tasty cheese. I don't think anyone will know the difference! I also like to use 'lite' cream.

Ann Turnbull

MINCE

Chop Suey

This is my son's favourite dish, so I had to submit the recipe for publication. I grew up eating this and still eat it to this day. It's easy to make and delicious to eat – a huge favourite in my household. Another wonderful family recipe to be passed on through the generations and to everyone.

Serves 4 • Preparation 15 mins • Cook 2 hours • Capacity 6 litres

500 g (1 lb 2 oz) minced (ground) beef
1 large onion, chopped
2 teaspoons curry powder, plus a little more
½ cabbage, chopped
2 cups frozen beans
2 carrots, diced
45 g (1½ oz) packet chicken noodle soup mix
Soy sauce, to taste
½ cup white rice

1. Brown the mince in a large non-stick frying pan, breaking up lumps with a wooden spoon. Add onion and curry powder, and cook, stirring occasionally, until tender. Drain off the excess fat. Transfer to the slow cooker.
2. Add the cabbage, beans, carrot, chicken noodle soup, soy sauce and a little bit more curry powder. Pour in 2 cups water and mix to combine.
3. Cover and cook on HIGH. Check after about 30 minutes. If the dish is looking a little watery, add some cornflour to thicken. Cook for a further 1.5 hours.
4. Close to serving time, cook the rice separately. Serve the chop suey on the rice.

Trinity Simmons

Curried Meatballs

My family loves a mild curry, and when budgets are tight, meatballs are a great meat to use in your curry. You can even make the meatballs in advance to save time. These have quite a curry kick to them (I would suggest medium heat). You could reduce the amount of curry powder in the sauce or serve without sauce for young ones or those who don't like too much heat.

Makes 22 meatballs • Preparation 15 mins • Cook 3 hours • Cooker capacity 5 litres

MEATBALLS

500 g (1 lb 2 oz) minced (ground) beef
½ onion, grated
1 egg
½ cup fine breadcrumbs
¼ teaspoon freshly ground black pepper

SAUCE

½ onion, grated
2 tablespoons tomato paste
2 tablespoons fruit chutney
1 tablespoon curry powder
2 teaspoons beef stock powder
Bow-tie pasta and green vegetables, to serve

1. To make the meatballs, use your hands to thoroughly combine all the ingredients. Wash your hands then use damp hands to roll into balls. They should be about golf ball sized.
2. Gently place the meatballs straight into the slow cooker. Combine all the sauce ingredients and 1½ cups hot water in a jug and pour gently over the meatballs.
3. Cover and cook on LOW for 3 hours (some slow cookers may need a little longer; just ensure meatballs are cooked through by testing one if you are not sure).
4. Just before serving, gently turn each meatball over in the sauce to ensure good coverage. Serve with pasta and vegetables.

NOTE: Meatballs could be made the night before and stored in the fridge if you prefer.

Paulene Christie

Cheesy Chicken Garlic Balls

If you are anything like me you know and love the garlic chicken balls you see in the hot box at your local corner shop. This is the closest I could get to recreating those bad boys – but with the addition of cheese inside. Eat these as a side or a main, or serve them at your next party.

Makes 16 balls • Preparation 15 mins • Cook 2 hours • Cooker capacity 7 litres

500 g (1 lb 2 oz) minced (ground) chicken
4 garlic cloves, minced
1 egg
¾ cup breadcrumbs
90 g (3 oz) tasty cheese, cut into 5 mm (¼ inch) cubes
Spray oil

1. Mix the chicken mince and garlic until combined. Lightly beat the egg in a bowl, and place the breadcrumbs into another bowl.
2. Take a slightly heaped tablespoon of chicken mince and press a cube of cheese into it. Shape the mince around the cheese to enclose and make a neat ball.
3. Roll each ball in egg, then in breadcrumbs to coat
4. Spray the slow cooker bowl lightly with oil (or line with baking paper). Place the balls into the slow cooker.
5. Cover, putting a tea towel (dish towel) under the lid, and cook on HIGH for up to 2 hours, turning balls after 45 minutes.

Simon Christie

My Sicilian Bolognaise

I came up with this recipe because my children adore my pasta dishes, and I wanted something hearty for colder days. I also wanted to make something Sicilian since that is my background.

Serves 6 • Preparation 10 mins • Cook 6 hours • Cooker capacity 5 litres

500 g (1 lb 2 oz) minced (ground) beef
1–2 tsp garlic powder
2 x 400g (14 oz) cans diced tomatoes (or a large jar of your favourite pasta sauce)
1 onion, chopped
1 chilli, deseeded and chopped
2 garlic cloves, minced
Handful each fresh basil and oregano
½ cup black olives, chopped
Pasta, to serve

1. Place the mince into the slow cooker and break up with a wooden spoon. Add the garlic powder and season with salt and pepper.
2. Pour the tomatoes over, and add the onion, chilli and garlic. Lay the herbs on top.
3. Cover and cook on LOW for 6 hours, stirring occasionally.
4. Just before serving, stir in the olives. Serve with pasta.

NOTE: If you want it extra tasty, about 15 minutes before serving add shredded mozzarella cheese and close the lid. This will melt on top of the meat, making it very tasty and irresistible!

Stephanie Watson

Mac & Beef

This is something I just threw together one day and we really enjoyed it. This recipe is very filling, easy to make and great for kids.

Serves 4–6 • Preparation 10 mins • Cook 1–2 hours • Cooker capacity 5 litres

500 g (1 lb 2 oz) minced (ground) beef
1 large onion, chopped
2 tablespoon minced garlic
700 g (1 lb 9 oz) bottle tomato passata (pureed tomato)
400g (14 oz) can diced tomatoes
200 g (7 oz) macaroni
2 tablespoons soy sauce
2 teaspoons dried Italian herbs

1. Brown the mince, onion and garlic in a large non-stick frying pan, breaking up lumps with a wooden spoon.
2. Transfer to the slow cooker and stir in the tomato passata, tomatoes, macaroni, soy sauce, herbs and 400 ml (13½ fl oz) water. Season with salt.
3. Cover and cook on HIGH for 1–2 hours, until the macaroni is tender.

NOTE: Sprinkle some grated cheese on top to make it a cheesy Mac and beef if you like.

Kaylah James

Classic Curried Mince

Unlike the curried mince packed with hidden vegetables on page 94, this is a classic curried mince that's very versatile. Serve it with creamy mash, cracked black pepper and a scattering of fresh chives, or use as a ready-made filling for curried pies, pasties or toasted sandwiches. You could also top with mashed potato or sweet potato and cheese for a curried cottage pie. Alternatively, serve with seasonal vegetables and crusty bread rolls. So many options for this budget mince base.

Serves 6 • Preparation 10 mins • Cook 5 hours • Cooker capacity 5 litres

1 kg (2 lb 3 oz) lean minced (ground) beef
1½ cups beef stock
1 large onion, diced
1 large carrot, finely diced
½ cup tomato sauce (ketchup)
2 tablespoons curry powder
1 tablespoon Worcestershire sauce
1 heaped teaspoon minced garlic
Cracked black pepper to taste

1. Combine all the ingredients in the slow cooker. Season with freshly cracked black pepper.
2. Cover and cook on LOW for 4–5 hours.

NOTE: If you like, combine 1 tablespoon cornflour with 1 tablespoon water until smooth. Stir into the beef mixture at the end of cooking to thicken.

Paulene Christie

Tom Soy

The name 'Tom Soy' came about from a version of San Choy Bow. I couldn't remember the name so I always called it Tom Soy.

Serves 4 • Preparation 10 mins • Cook 2 hours • Cooker capacity 6 litres

2 teaspoons oil
1 brown onion, chopped
3–4 mushroom cups, chopped
1–2 cm (½ inch) piece fresh ginger, finely grated
2 teaspoons minced garlic
500 g (1 lb 2 oz) minced (ground) pork
½ cup sweet chilli sauce
⅓ cup oyster sauce
2 teaspoons soy sauce
½ tsp fish sauce
1 cup rice vermicelli noodles
Handful chopped spring onions (scallions)
Lettuce leaves, to serve

1. Heat oil in a frying pan and add the onion, mushrooms, ginger and garlic. Cook over medium heat for a few minutes, to caramelise.
2. Add to the slow cooker, along with the pork and sauces. Stir to combine.
3. Cover and cook on LOW for 2 hours.
4. Place the noodles into a heatproof bowl and cover with boiling water. Stand for 5 minutes, to soften. Drain and add to the pork mixture. Add spring onions.
5. Serve mixture in lettuce leaf cups.

Tennille Langley

Minced Beef Hash

A really tasty, family-friendly meal. It's my take on the potato gem casserole, as in England we don't have those! It can easily be bulked out with lots of veggies.

Serves 4–6 • Preparation 15 mins • Cook 3½ hours • Cooker capacity 6.5 litres

500 g (1 lb 2 oz) lean minced (ground) beef
400g (14 oz) can diced tomatoes
420 g (15 oz) can condensed tomato soup
1 onion, diced
2 heaped teaspoons minced garlic
1 beef stock cube, dissolved in ½ cup hot water
2 heaped teaspoons beef gravy granules
1 teaspoon English mustard
Generous dash Worcestershire sauce
10 frozen hash browns
150 g (5½ oz) grated tasty cheese

1. Combine the mince, tomatoes, soup, onion, garlic, stock, gravy granules, mustard and Worcestershire sauce in a bowl. Use your hands to mix evenly.
2. Transfer mixture to the slow cooker and top with hash browns.
3. Cover and cook on LOW for 3½–6 hours.
4. Sprinkle cheese evenly over the top, and replace lid with a tea towel (dish towel) underneath. Cook for 30 minutes.

NOTE: For extra richness melt the stock cube in warmed red wine.

Joanne Pinnock

Mild Mexican Mince In Minutes

This is a great versatile mince that can be used as the base of all your favourite Mexican meals, such as tacos, nachos, enchiladas and taco salads, or even as a baked potato topper. It's fast to assemble and foolproof to cook. It also freezes well for later use, so why not make a double batch and save some for a busy night ahead?

Serves 6 • Preparation 5 mins • Cook 4–5 hours • Cooker capacity 5 litres

500 g (1 lb 2 oz) lean minced (ground) beef
500 g (1 lb 2 oz) mixed diced frozen (or fresh) vegetables
30 g (1 oz) packet taco seasoning mix

1. Combine all the ingredients in the slow cooker. Add 1 cup water and stir to combine.
2. Cover and cook on LOW for 4–5 hours.

Paulene Christie

Slap Together Chilli Con Carne

'Slap together' is what this recipe is all about! One day I just 'slapped together' what I had in my pantry. It's not really chilli con carne – it's more a mixture of that with a taco mince type dish.

Serves 4 • Preparation 10 mins • Cook 3 hours • Cooker capacity 3.5 litres

500 g (1 lb 2 oz) minced (ground) beef
400 g (14 oz) can salt-reduced chickpeas, rinsed and drained
400 g (14 oz) can red kidney beans, rinsed and drained
300g jar mild (or chunky) salsa
2 tomatoes, chopped
1 carrot, finely chopped
1 garlic clove, minced
1 teaspoon chilli flakes
1 teaspoon ground cumin
1 teaspoon cinnamon
1 teaspoon paprika
¼ teaspoon ground black pepper
Corn chips and Greek yoghurt, to serve

1. Brown the mince in a large non-stick frying pan, breaking up lumps with a wooden spoon. Drain off the excess fat. Transfer to the slow cooker.
2. Mix the chickpeas, kidney beans, salsa, tomatoes, carrot, garlic and ½ cup water together in a bowl. Combine the spices in a small bowl, then stir into the tomato mixture. Season with salt and pour over the mince.
3. Cover and cook on HIGH for 3 hours.
4. Serve with corn chips and Greek yoghurt

NOTE: Alternatively, serve with rice and naan bread. Adding a squeeze of lime over the top gives a little tang to the flavour.

Roslyn Potter

Savoury Mince

This savoury mince is perfect with pasta rice or even wrapped up in some puff pastry. It's a very versatile dish.

Serves 6–8 • Preparation 15 mins • Cook 4 hours • Cooker capacity 5 litres

1 kg (2 lb 3 oz) minced (ground) beef
1 teaspoon minced garlic
3–4 cups beef stock
2 carrots, diced
2 onions, diced
1 cup frozen mixed peas and corn, thawed
½ cup BBQ sauce
⅓ cup sweet chilli sauce
¼ cup Worcestershire sauce
¼ cup tomato sauce (ketchup)
Vegetables and rice or pasta, to serve

1. Heat a large non-stick frying pan and add the mince and garlic. Cook over medium-high heat, breaking up lumps with a wooden spoon, until browned.
2. Transfer to the slow cooker and add the remaining ingredients. Season with salt and pepper.
3. Cover and cook on HIGH for 4 hours.
4. Serve with vegetables and rice or pasta.

Kassandra Carter

2-minute-noodle Spaghetti

My mum made this for me when I was younger and now I make it. Being a mum of three kids I find it's so easy and budget friendly!

Serves 4–6 • Preparation 5 mins • Cook 6 hours • Cooker capacity 5.5 litres

1 onion, chopped
500 g (1 lb 2 oz) minced (ground) beef
2 x 500 g (1 lb 2 oz) jars pasta sauce
2 x 74 g (2½ oz) packets 2-minute noodles

1. Place the onion into the slow cooker. Add the mince and break up with a wooden spoon, then add the remaining ingredients.
2. Cover and cook on LOW for 6 hours, stirring regularly during the last 2 hours.

NOTE: Alternatively, you can cook the noodles in the microwave and put them into the slow cooker closer to the end. Feel free to add your own herbs and spices.

Jessica Rowlands

Chow Mein Mince

We love chow mein mince, but we needed to cut down on salt so I decided to make my own. Using spices I already keep on hand, I came up with this cheap and easy option that my children love.

Serves 4–6 • Preparation 10 mins • Cook 2½ hours • Cooker capacity 7 litres

1 kg (2 lb 3 oz) minced (ground) beef
1 cup long-grain rice, rinsed well
2 medium carrots, thinly sliced
1–2 tablespoons curry powder (depending on taste)
1 tablespoon chicken stock powder (salt-reduced if you like)
1 teaspoon onion powder
1 teaspoon ground cumin
½ teaspoon ground ginger
½ cabbage, shredded

1. Brown the mince in a large non-stick frying pan, breaking up lumps with a wooden spoon. Drain off the excess fat. Transfer to the slow cooker.
2. Add the rice, carrots, curry powder, stock powder, onion powder, cumin, ginger and 2 cups water. Stir to combine.
3. Cover and cook on HIGH for 2 hours, until rice is almost tender.
4. Spread cabbage over the top and cook for 15 minutes, until cabbage wilts. Stir to combine and cook for a further 15 minutes, until rice and cabbage are tender.

NOTE: If you use basmati rice decrease the cooking time by around ½ an hour.

Karen Stuckings

Curried Mince – Vegetable Loaded

This is a great way to incorporate lots of vegetables into your dish and who doesn't love that! Cooking it all together means less mess and less fuss. You could make this go even further if you wanted, by serving it with vegetable mash or rice on the side.

Serves 6 • Preparation 15 mins • Cook 4–5 hours • Cooker capacity 5 litres

1 kg (2 lb 3 oz) minced (ground) beef
400 g (14 oz) can diced tomatoes (or diced fresh tomatoes)
1 onion, diced
2 carrots, grated
1 zucchini, diced
1 medium eggplant, diced
½ cup dried green peas
2 teaspoons minced garlic
¼ cup tomato paste (concentrated puree)
1 tablespoon curry powder
2 teaspoons beef stock powder
Bread rolls, creamy mashed potato or sweet potato mash, to serve

1. Place the mince into the slow cooker and break up with a wooden spoon. Add the vegetables and stir to combine.
2. Combine the tomato paste, curry powder, stock powder and 1 cup warm water in a jug. Pour into the slow cooker and mix well.
3. Cover and cook on LOW for 4–5 hours.
4. Serve with bread rolls, creamy mashed potato or sweet potato mash.

Paulene Christie

Italian Meatball Subs

This is a recipe we created during sports season when our children were playing night games over dinner time. So much more affordable than buying food for a large family at the fields and more nutritious too! It's also great for parties: you can serve the meatballs right from the slow cooker, and guests can just assemble their subs as they want them.

Makes 28 meatballs • Preparation 15 mins • Cook 4–5 hours • Cooker capacity 6 litres

MEATBALLS

600 g (1 lb 5 oz) minced (ground) pork and veal (70% pork, 30% veal)
1 egg
1 tablespoon chopped fresh parsley
½ teaspoon salt
1 teaspoon minced garlic
1½ tablespoons finely grated parmesan cheese
⅓ cup panko breadcrumbs

SAUCE

400 g (14 oz) can diced tomatoes with herbs and tomato paste (see note)
1 onion, finely diced
1 tablespoon minced garlic
1 tablespoon chopped fresh basil
1 tablespoon chopped fresh oregano
1 tablespoon chopped fresh parsley
Split hot dog rolls and parmesan cheese, to serve

1. To make the meatballs, use your hands to thoroughly combine all the meatball ingredients. Wash your hands then use damp hands to roll the mixture into balls. They should be smaller than a golf ball.
2. Combine all the sauce ingredients in the slow cooker. Gently place meatballs on top of sauce, but do not stir.
3. Cover and cook on LOW for 4–5 hours.
4. Serve in hot dog rolls, sprinkled with parmesan.

NOTE: Resist the urge to touch the meatballs at all until at least the last hour, so they remain firmly intact. I flip them over gently in the last hour then leave them again.

If you can't purchase the tomatoes combined with herbs and paste, use a 400 g can of diced tomatoes combined with 1 teaspoon dried mixed herbs and 1 tablespoon tomato paste (concentrated puree).

Paulene Christie

Lasagne

This is a family recipe that I adapted for the slow cooker.

Serves 4 • Preparation 20 mins • Cook 3½ hours • Cooker capacity 5 litres

Spray oil
Lasagne sheets (dry) (see note)
1–2 cups grated mozzarella cheese
¼–½ cup grated parmesan cheese

MEAT SAUCE
1 tablespoon olive oil
1 kg (2 lb 3 oz) minced (ground) beef
2 onions, diced
200 g (7 oz) mushrooms, chopped
2 garlic cloves, minced
2 teaspoons dried oregano
2 teaspoons dried basil
2 x 400 g (14 oz) cans diced tomatoes
280 g (10 oz) tomato paste
120 g (4½ oz) baby spinach leaves

MICROWAVE BÉCHAMEL SAUCE
40 g (1½ oz) butter
2 tablespoons plain (all-purpose) flour
600 ml (20½ fl oz) milk

1. To make the meat sauce, heat the oil in a large frying pan over medium-high heat. Add the mince, onion, mushrooms, garlic and herbs. Cook for about 5 minutes or until lightly browned, using a wooden spoon to break up lumps of mince. Add the tomatoes, tomato paste and spinach. Season with salt and pepper, and stir to combine. Set aside.
2. To make the microwave bechamel sauce, place the butter into a large microwave-safe bowl. Microwave for about 30 seconds, until melted. Stir in the flour and cook for 1 minute, until it resembles breadcrumbs. Stir in the milk and cook in 1 minute bursts until thick, stirring between each burst (about 3 minutes in total). Season with salt and pepper.
3. To assemble, lightly spray the slow cooker bowl with oil. Make a layer of the meat sauce in the bowl, and top with a layer of bechamel and a sprinkle of mozzarella. Arrange a single layer of lasagne sheets over the bechamel. Cover liberally with another layer of meat sauce and bechamel. Sprinkle with mozzarella.
4. Continue layering, finishing with a layer of bechamel topped with mozzarella and parmesan.
5. Cover, putting a tea towel (dish towel) under the lid, and cook on HIGH for 2 hours then reduce to LOW and cook for 1½ hours.

NOTE: The number of lasagne sheets depends on how many layers you would like to make. Also, you can double the bechamel if you like a creamy lasagne.

Melissa McClelland

Meatball Subs

This is my go-to recipe: the kids love it and I can throw it together quickly before we are out the door. It's very cheap to make and goes a long way.

Serves 6 • Preparation 15 mins • Cook 6 hours • Cooker capacity 6 litres

1 kg (2 lb 3 oz) minced (ground) beef
1 egg
½ cup breadcrumbs
2 tablespoons soy sauce
2 tablespoons Worcestershire sauce
40 g (1½ oz) packet French onion soup mix
1 heaped teaspoon minced garlic
Good dash sesame oil
Handful chopped fresh flat-leaf parsley, plus extra for top
Plain (all-purpose) flour, to coat
1 tablespoon olive oil
2 x 420 g (15 oz) cans pasta sauce (about 3 cups)
12 long bread rolls, split along the top and buttered
Grated tasty cheese, for topping
Salad or hot chips, to serve

1. Combine the mince, egg, breadcrumbs, sauces, soup mix, garlic, sesame oil and parsley in a bowl. Season with salt and pepper and mix with your hands until well combined.
2. Roll into balls about the size of a golf ball (picture fitting about 4 into each long bread roll). Toss in flour to coat, and shake off excess.
3. Heat oil in a large frying pan and cook meatballs until just browned. Transfer to the slow cooker in a single layer. Pour the pasta sauce over the meatballs. Season with salt and pepper and sprinkle with extra parsley.
4. Cover and cook on LOW for 4 hours.
5. Add 4 meatballs and some sauce to each roll. Sprinkle tops with cheese and pop under the grill to melt the cheese.

NOTE: Browning the meatballs helps to hold them together during cooking. Don't stir the meatballs when cooking, because this can cause them to break apart. This makes a lot of meatballs so I normally reserve about 15 from cooking for the next night to have with pasta.

Katherine Barron

Cheesy Mexican Mince

The best thing about this dish is all the many meals you can create with it! It's a great budget base that you don't need a lot of per serve. As a bonus you could then eat it two nights in a row without feeling like you are eating the same meal twice. It makes the second night's dinner so easy! Eat Mexican at home without the take-away costs!

Serves 6 • Preparation 5 mins • Cook 4 hours • Cooker capacity 5 litres

1 kg (2 lb 3 oz) lean minced (ground) beef
375 g (13 oz) jar enchilada sauce
200 g (7 oz) jar mild chunky salsa
1 small green capsicum (pepper), finely diced
35 g (1 oz) packet taco seasoning mix
1½ cups grated tasty cheese

1. Combine all the ingredients except the cheese and add to the slow cooker. Press down and spread out the mixture evenly.
2. Cover and cook on LOW for 3½ hours.
3. Sprinkle the cheese over the mixture. Cover, putting a tea towel (dish towel) under the lid, and cook for a further 30 minutes, for the cheese to melt.

NOTE: You could increase the heat of the spice by using spicy salsa and enchilada sauce instead of mild.

The serving options are many: as filling for tacos, tortillas or enchiladas, in wraps, lettuce cups or in salads, or on bread rolls with salad. It's also nice with a dollop of sour cream and a side salad

Paulene Christie

Macaroni Meatballs in Minutes

The entire purpose of this meal is to make it in minutes. For this recipe we are dealing with the raw, ready-made meatballs that you can buy from the supermarket. Sure you can make your own meatballs (I usually do for other recipes), but this one is specifically for those days you literally have no time. We all have those days! That's often a day we are tempted to turn to take-away so this is a much more budget friendly option. It's a one pot meal that is served straight from your slow cooker so you have the added bonus of less washing-up too.

Serves 6 • Preparation 5 mins • Cook 4½ hours • Cooker capacity 5 litres

800 g (1 lb 12 oz) ready-made small meatballs
700 g (1 lb 9 oz) bottle pasta sauce
250 g (7 oz) macaroni
Grated parmesan or tasty cheese, to serve

1. Place the meatballs into the slow cooker and pour over the pasta sauce. Don't stir, as they will fall apart.
2. Cover and cook on LOW for 4 hours.
3. Add the macaroni and 1¼ cups boiling water and stir gently to combine. Cook for a further 30 minutes or until pasta is tender. Don't worry if it looks watery; the pasta will absorb much of the liquid. If it dries out too much you can always add a splash more hot water.
4. Serve straight from the slow cooker, with a scattering of grated cheese.

NOTE: You can cook the pasta separately if you prefer and stir it through just before serving.

You can also use ready-cooked meatballs, reduce the cooking time to 2 hours.

Paulene Christie

Mum's Mexican Mince

I make a huge batch of this and serve it up with brown rice one night, and with tortillas or taco shells the next. My boys absolutely LOVE it.

Serves 4–6 (for 2 meals) • Preparation 10 mins • Cook 6–8 hours • Cooker capacity 6 litres

2 kg (4 lb 6 oz) minced (ground) beef
1 onion, chopped
30 g (1 oz) packet taco seasoning mix
400 g (14 oz) can diced tomatoes
400 g (14 oz) can red kidney beans, rinsed and drained
420 g (15 oz) can corn kernels, drained
1 green capsicum (pepper), chopped
Brown rice, tortillas or taco shells, to serve

1. Place the mince into the slow cooker and break up with a wooden spoon. Add the onion, sprinkle with taco seasoning and pour the tomatoes over. Stir in the beans and corn, and season with salt and pepper.
2. Cover and cook on LOW for 5–7 hours.
3. Add the capsicum and cook for a further 1 hour.
4. Serve with brown rice, tortillas or taco shells.

NOTE: You can add any extras you like to this dish. I often add a grated carrot or some peas. I ALWAYS add extra chilli to my serve because I like it hot!

Fiona Masters

Cheesy Chicken & Chorizo Ravioli

Don't have the time or inclination to make your own ravioli? You don't need to! We've created this recipe for you to use easily with ready-made ravioli. Choose whichever kind of ravioli you like best to form the base of this dish, and with a few extra steps you have a delicious pasta dish served with a chicken mince and chorizo sauce. If your ravioli better suits beef flavours you could swap the chicken mince for lean beef mince, which will cut the budget down even further.

Serves 6 • Preparation 15 mins • Cook 4½ hours • Cooker capacity 5 litres

1 tablespoon olive oil
500 g (1 lb 2 oz) minced (ground) chicken
250 g (9 oz) chorizo sausage, diced
785 g (1 lb 11½ oz) bottle pasta sauce (I used tomato, onion and roasted garlic)
400 g (14 oz) can diced tomatoes
625 g (1 lb 6 oz) packet fresh ravioli (I used roast chicken and garlic)
200 g (7 oz) grated mozzarella cheese
Garden salad and crusty garlic bread, to serve

1. Heat the oil in a searing slow cooker (or frying pan on the stovetop over medium-high heat) and cook the chicken mince and chorizo, breaking up lumps with a wooden spoon, until browned.
2. Combine mince, chorizo, pasta sauce and tomatoes in the slow cooker.
3. Cover and cook on LOW for 4 hours.
4. Add the ravioli and stir to combine. Cook for 15 minutes, then sprinkle with cheese and cook for a further 15 minutes.
5. Serve with garden salad and crusty garlic bread.

NOTE: Ravioli could be replaced with tortellini if you desire. You can also vary the filling of the pasta you choose to suit your tastes.

Paulene Christie

SAUSAGES

Currywurst

I went to Germany two years ago and came across currywurst at the food stalls at music festivals. It is so good. When I came home I had really bad cravings for it and as there are no currywurst stands here, I looked up recipes online and I made it myself before I had a slow cooker. Now I've converted the old recipe to a slow cooker version and it tastes just like the real thing in Germany. Prost!

Serves 4 • Preparation 10 mins • Cook 2 hours • Cooker capacity 5.5 litres

1 cup passata (pureed tomato)
1 cup tomato sauce (ketchup)
1 small onion, finely chopped
1 tablespoon curry powder, plus extra to serve
1 tsp ground cumin
1 tsp ground paprika
8 pork sausages
Hot chips, to serve

1. Combine the passata, sauce, onion, curry powder, spices and ½ cup water in the slow cooker, then add the sausages.
2. Cover and cook on HIGH for 1½ hours.
3. Take the sausages out and cut into bite-sized pieces. Return to the slow cooker and cook for a further 30 minutes.
4. Serve with a sprinkle of curry powder on top, along with chips.

NOTE: For traditional German currywurst, try weisswurst (white sausages). You could also use pork chipolatas.

Keith Hechinger

Honey Balsamic Sausages

I adapted this from my oven recipe. It's easy and full of flavour.

Serves 4 • Preparation 10 mins • Cook 6–8 hours • Cooker capacity 3.5 litres

1 onion, sliced
⅓ cup honey
⅓ cup balsamic vinegar
8 sausages
400 g (14 oz) can green lentils, rinsed and drained

1. Place the onion into the slow cooker. Pour over the honey and balsamic vinegar.
2. Place the sausages on top, then pour the lentils over the sausages.
3. Cover and cook on LOW for 6–8 hours.

NOTE: If you can get them, Lincolnshire sausages are great in this.

Joanne Pinnock

Curried Sausages

This is my beautiful Nan's recipe. Every time I make it, I think about her and staying at her house on school holidays when she would always make this for us!

Serves 4 • Preparation 15 mins • Cook 6–8 hours • Cooker capacity 5 litres

8 sausages
1 onion, chopped
½ cup long grain rice
2 carrots, chopped
3 celery stalks, chopped
1 small apple, chopped
1 banana, chopped
1 tomato, peeled and chopped
½ green capsicum (pepper), chopped
1 teaspoon curry powder
1 teaspoon dried oregano
1 teaspoon sugar
1 beef and 1 chicken stock cube (or 1 teaspoon each stock powder)
Pinch ground cumin
Rice or mashed potato, to serve

1. Cook sausages in a saucepan of boiling water for about 5 minutes, until skins fall off. Cut each sausage into about 6 pieces.
2. Combine all the ingredients in the slow cooker, along with 3 cups water.
3. Cover and cook on LOW for 6–8 hours, adding 1 more cup water halfway through cooking if required. Season with salt and pepper.
4. Serve with rice or mashed potato or enjoy as is.

NOTE: It is best to boil the sausages first, so the skins don't come off into the sauce.

Melissa McClelland

Sausages All In

Sausages are cheap so I am always looking for new ways to cook with them. That's how the idea of 'Sausages all in' was born. It's a combination of a memory of a dish that I used to enjoy as a kid and the flavours my family enjoys now.

Serves 5 • Preparation 10 mins • Cook 4–5 hours • Cooker capacity 6 litres

500 g (1 lb 2 oz) sausages
2 x 400 g (14 oz) cans diced tomatoes
1 onion, diced
1 sweet potato, cubed
2 teaspoons minced garlic
½ teaspoon mustard powder
½ teaspoon mild paprika
Mashed potato, to serve

1. Put everything into the slow cooker and stir to combine.
2. Cover and cook on LOW for 4–5 hours.
3. Season with salt and pepper, and serve with mashed potato.

NOTE: If you prefer, you can cook for 2 hours, take out the sausages and cut them up, put them back in the slow cooker and cook for a further 2–3 hours. You can add any vegetables that you want.

Bel Ruddy

Loaded Beans

This is a perfect cheap, quick meal to end or start a busy day! In my home, we use it for nights when the kids have sport, and I need a meal I know will get eaten quickly with no fuss. Knowing it's bubbling away in the slow cooker stops the take-away run on the way home. Leftovers are for brekky the next morning.

Serves 3–4 • Preparation 5 mins • Cook 4 hours • Cooker capacity 6 litres

2 x 420 g (15 oz) cans baked beans
400 g (14 oz) can diced tomatoes
400 g (14 oz) can cocktail franks, drained
1 onion, finely diced

1. Place all the ingredients into the slow cooker and stir well to combine.
2. Cover and cook on LOW for 4 hours, stirring occasionally.

NOTE: The canned franks can be replaced with cocktail franks from the deli, but I find the canned ones to be more cost effective, and also easier to eat with a spoon. The recipe can be doubled or tripled easily without modifying the cooking time.

Sarah Jenkins

Chilli, Chorizo & Green Bean Spaghetti

This cheap and cheerful meal is a regular favourite in our house (we usually have a side salad too just to get extra veggies into the kids). Sadly, there are never leftovers for lunch the next day!

Serves 4–6 • Preparation 10 mins • Cook 6 hours • Cooker capacity 6 litres

2 chorizo sausages
2 x 400 g (14 oz) cans diced tomatoes
1 onion, chopped
1 tablespoon minced garlic
1 teaspoon dried chilli flakes (optional)
1 teaspoon dried Italian herbs
2 cups frozen green beans
Spaghetti, grated parmesan cheese and sweet chilli sauce, to serve

1. Cut the chorizo in half lengthways, then chop into bite-sized pieces. Combine the chorizo in the slow cooker with the tomatoes, onion, garlic, chilli and herbs.
2. Cover and cook on LOW for 4 hours, then add the beans and cook for another 2 hours.
3. Serve on a bed of spaghetti, with a sprinkle of parmesan and some sweet chilli sauce.

NOTE: Beans can be added at the start but they lose a bit of crunch and colour when cooked for a long time. Chorizo is often on special (usually half price) at the deli section of our local supermarket, so I stock up then because it freezes well. Just remember always to defrost meat completely before adding it to the slow cooker.

Fiona Masters

Devilled Sausages

This is a lovely hot dish that I serve on those cold winter nights in New Zealand. I love it because it's very cheap and my toddler loves it.

Serves 2–4 • Preparation 10 mins • Cook 3 hours • Cooker capacity 3 litres

500 g (1 lb 2 oz) beef sausages, cut into pieces
1 large onion, sliced
About 8 mushrooms (optional)
1 cup tomato sauce (ketchup)

1. Combine the sausages and onion in the slow cooker. Add the mushrooms (if using), sauce and ½ cup water.
2. Cover and cook on LOW for 3 hours.

Jane Corbett

Sausage Obsession

Lamb Obsession (from *Slow Cooker Central* book 1) is by far my most popular recipe, but I understand that for some people lamb just doesn't fit in the budget. Enter Sausage Obsession! Using budget sausages saves heaps off the cost of the original recipe. It's also less oily and has no bones to worry about. If you are using a sausage type other than lamb you may choose to omit the mint sauce, but I tend to leave it in regardless because it's part of the overall 'Obsession' flavour I know and love.

Serves 6 • Preparation 10 mins • Cook 4 hours • Cooker capacity 5 litres

12 thin lamb or beef sausages
1 brown onion, diced
420 g (15 oz) can condensed cream of mushroom soup
40 g (1½ oz) packet French onion soup mix
1–2 tablespoons Worcestershire sauce
1 tablespoon mint sauce or mint jelly (optional)

1. Place the sausages into the slow cooker and add the onion.
2. Combine the other ingredients and pour over the sausages.
3. Cover and cook on LOW for about 4 hours.

Paulene Christie

Sweet Sausage Curry

Sausages are such a versatile meat for those on a budget. So many recipes that use other meats can be made with sausages instead, and a curry is no different. This serves our family of five with leftovers for at least another two serves. It's great for the budget and great to fill hungry tummies at the end of a long day. Serve with creamy mashed potato for a filling meal that won't break the bank.

Serves 8 • Preparation 15 mins • Cook 5 hours • Cooker capacity 6 litres

16 thin beef sausages
2 onions, diced
2 small Granny Smith apples, peeled, cored and diced
1½ cups beef stock
⅔ cup fruit chutney
3 teaspoons mild curry powder
2 garlic cloves, minced
½ teaspoon minced ginger
Mashed potato and steamed vegetables, to serve

1. Cut the sausages into chunks (about 6 pieces per sausage). Place the sausages, onion and apple into the slow cooker.
2. Combine the other ingredients, mixing well, and pour into the slow cooker.
3. Cover and cook on LOW for 5 hours.
4. Serve with mashed potato and vegetables.

Paulene Christie

Sausage Casserole

I make budget meals to help my neighbour who has battled breast cancer. She has a husband who works hard and two young primary school boys. I know the last couple of years have taken their toll on the family. I have become quite inventive in cooking for them – here is one of the inventions I have come up with.

Serves 8 • Preparation 15 mins • Cook 5 hours • Cooker capacity 5–6 litres

12 sausages, cut into pieces
¼ cup plain (all-purpose) flour
600 ml (20½ fl oz) tomato sauce (ketchup) or BBQ sauce
400 g (14 oz) can diced tomatoes
1 onion, chopped
40 g (1½ oz) packet French onion soup mix
3 garlic cloves, minced
Vegetables, chopped (use a variety, enough so slow cooker is about ⅔ full)
Pasta, to serve

1. Place the sausage pieces and flour into the slow cooker and toss to coat.
2. Add the remaining ingredients and stir to combine.
3. Cover and cook on HIGH for 5 hours. Serve with pasta.

NOTE: Use vegetables that are cheap and in season. I use zucchini, carrots, beans, pumpkin, celery, cauliflower, potatoes and sweet potatoes. You can omit the pasta if including potatoes.

Chistine Mcinnes

Sausage Bolognese

This recipe is a super simple tasty one that's good for end of week meals before pay day, or just when motivation is low. It's cheap, easy to make and has delicious flavours.

Serves 6 • Preparation 10 mins • Cook 5–6 hours • Capacity 5.5 litres

8–12 sausages
700 g (1 lb 9 oz) bottle passata (pureed tomato)
400 g (14 oz) can diced tomatoes with herbs
¼–½ cup fresh basil leaves
¼–½ cup fresh oregano leaves
Pasta or crusty bread, to serve

1. Cook the sausages in a saucepan of boiling water for about 5 minutes, until skins fall off (this is optional, I just prefer the texture).
2. Transfer sausages to the slow cooker and mix in the passata, tomatoes and herbs.
3. Cover and cook on LOW for 5–6 hours. About 30 minutes before they are ready chop sausages into bite-sized pieces and put back into slow cooker.
4. Serve over pasta or with bread.

NOTE: The taste can be rich so add less basil and oregano for a milder flavour if you prefer.

Michelle Halfpenny

Summer Sausage Braise

This braised sausage dish is lovely, with light summer flavours of cherry tomatoes and celery.

Serves 6–8 • Preparation 10 mins • Cook 6 hours • Cooker capacity 5.5 litres

1 tablespoon olive oil
12–14 chicken or pork sausages
10 small onions
250 g (9 oz) chopped bacon
500 g (1 lb 2 oz) cherry tomatoes
150 ml (5½ fl oz) dry white wine
150 ml (5½ fl oz) vegetable stock
3 celery stalks, chopped
3 garlic cloves, minced
Crusty bread and salad, to serve

1. Heat the olive oil in a large frying pan over medium heat. Brown the sausages and add to the slow cooker. Add the onions and bacon to the frying pan and cook until brown, then transfer to the slow cooker.
2. Mix in the tomatoes, wine, stock, celery and garlic.
3. Cover and cook on LOW for 6 hours.
4. Season with salt and pepper, and serve with crusty bread and salad.

Lynda Eagleson

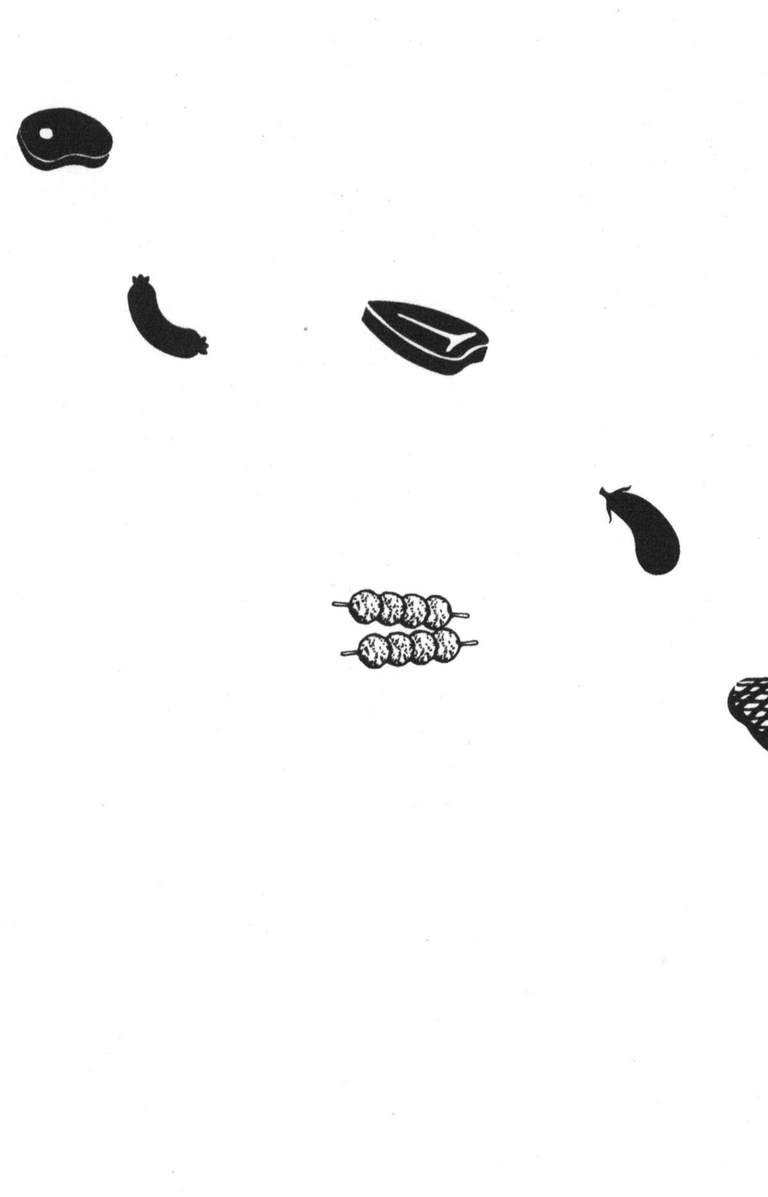

BEEF

Pickled Beef Tongue

Tongue is so cheap and versatile I thought I would try to cook it in the slow cooker. For the price of regular corned beef you can usually buy two or three tongues – very cost effective.

Serves 6 • Preparation 5 mins • Cook 6–8 hours • Cooker capacity 6 litres

1 large pickled beef tongue
¼ cup white vinegar
1 teaspoon crushed black pepper
1 teaspoon brown sugar
1 teaspoon garlic salt
2 dried bay leaves
Sprinkle of dried dill
Vegetables and mustard white sauce, to serve

1. Combine all the ingredients in the slow cooker and add enough water to cover completely.
2. Cover and cook on HIGH for 2 hours, then reduce to LOW and cook for 4–6 hours, until the tongue is very tender when tested with a knife.
3. Remove from cooking liquid and peel off outer layer. Serve with vegetables and sauce.

NOTE: Use leftovers in sandwiches or to make fritters, or any way you would use corned beef.

Kaz Dunemann

Hawaiian Steak

This is an old family favourite that got handed down from my great nan.

Serves 4 • Preparation 10 mins • Cook time 4 or 8 hours • Cooker capacity 5 litres

500 g (1 lb 2 oz) stewing steak, cut into bite-sized pieces
440 g (15½ oz) can crushed pineapple
420 g (15 oz) can condensed tomato soup
400 g (14 oz) can diced tomatoes

1. Place the steak into the slow cooker, and season with salt and pepper if you like.
2. Pour in the pineapple, soup and tomatoes. Stir until combined, adding a little water if you think it is needed.
3. Cover and cook on HIGH for 4 hours or LOW for 8 hours.

NOTE: You can also add some cooked mixed veggies at the end. I have found that minted peas are a wonderful addition.

Amber Philpott

Creamy Mushroom & Beef

I love experimenting while cooking and coming up with new ideas for our meals, and you probably do too, especially when budgeting to feed your family. I love the challenge of making my own new signature dish, and when hubby has that first mouthful at dinner time and says, "That's absolutely delicious, love," I know I have a winner and that puts a smile on my dial!

Serves 4 • Preparation 10 mins • Cook 6–8 hours • Cooker capacity 6 litres

500 g (1 lb 2 oz) stewing steak, diced
1 large onion, sliced
420 g (15 oz) can condensed cream of mushroom soup
1 cup sliced mushrooms
2 teaspoon minced garlic
1 tablespoon hot sauce
2 teaspoons chicken stock (powder)
300 ml (10½ fl oz) thickened (whipping) cream
Steamed rice or mashed potato, to serve

1. Combine the beef, onion, soup, mushrooms, garlic, hot sauce and stock in the slow cooker.
2. Cover and cook on LOW for 6–8 hours.
3. Just before serving, stir in the cream. Season with salt and pepper to taste. Serve with rice or mashed potato.

NOTE: You might like to try other cuts of meat, such as lamb forequarter chops.

Judith Clark

Lemonade Silverside

This recipe was inspired by the ginger beer silverside recipe I've always enjoyed. The lemonade is a nice alternative for those who don't like ginger. This version has a mild hint of sweetness to the meat but is still super tender because of the carbonation in the drink! It's also great with sugar-free lemonade or even sparkling mineral water for a low sugar, low carb alternative.

Serves 6 • Preparation 5 mins • Cook 8 hours • Cooker capacity 5 litres

1.5 kg (3 lb 5 oz) piece silverside
1.25 litres lemonade

1. Rinse the silverside and place into the slow cooker.
2. Pour in the lemonade – it's okay if it doesn't fully cover the silverside. You can always turn it halfway through cooking if you wish.
3. Cover and cook on LOW for 8 hours.

NOTE: This is lovely served with mashed potato, seasonal vegetables and a lush cheese sauce or white sauce

Paulene Christie

Mild Mexican Beef

A slow cooked, versatile Mexican mince – so easy and tasty! This is extremely mild to suit our whole family, but if you like it spicy then add fresh chillies or dried chilli flakes to suit your taste.

Serves 6–8 • Preparation 10 mins • Cook 5 hours • Cooker capacity 5.5 litres

1 kg (2 lb 3 oz) diced, sliced or minced (ground) beef
400 g (14 oz) can corn kernels, drained
2 large tomatoes, roughly chopped
1 large red onion, diced
4 large garlic cloves, sliced
2½ teaspoons sweet paprika
1 teaspoon ground cumin
1 teaspoon dried oregano
Pinch each salt and pepper
Sour cream and coriander (cilantro), to serve

1. Place the beef into the slow cooker. Add the corn, tomatoes, onion and garlic on top of the beef.
2. Sprinkle the paprika, cumin, oregano and salt and pepper over everything.
3. Cook on LOW for 5 hours.
4. Give the beef a good stir and serve with sour cream and coriander.

NOTE: You can serve this with your choice of bread rolls, rice, coleslaw or corn chips (which I like to heat in a 180°C/350°F oven for about 10 minutes).

Felicity Barnett

Silverside

This recipe was handed down from my mother and has been cooked many times over the years. Leftovers are always good for fritters, or just as cold meat!

Serves 4–6 (with leftovers) • Prep time 10 mins • Cook 6 hours • Cooker capacity 4 or 6 litres

1.5 kg (3 lb 5 oz) piece silverside
1 onion, roughly chopped
1 carrot, roughly chopped
¼ cup vinegar
1 tablespoon brown sugar
1 heaped teaspoon mustard powder
1 heaped teaspoon ground nutmeg
12 black peppercorns
6 whole cloves
2 bay leaves
¼ teaspoon ground allspice
2 tablespoons chutney

1. Place the silverside into the slow cooker, and add enough cold water to half-fill (the meat won't be completely covered).
2. Add the peppercorns, cloves, vinegar, brown sugar, bay leaves, mustard powder, nutmeg, allspice, onion and carrot. Brush the top of the silverside with chutney.
3. Cover and cook on HIGH for 4 hours, then reduce to LOW and cook for 2 hours.
4. Remove silverside from the slow cooker and stand for 10 minutes before slicing.

NOTE: Serve with white sauce, cheesy cauliflower, boiled potatoes, baby carrots and greens, with lashings of butter and tomato sauce.

Lorelei Doyle

Steak Diane

Steak Diane is one of my favourite dishes – the garlic mushroom sauce is divine. I use chuck steak and it just melts in your mouth.

Serves 6 • Preparation 10 mins • Cook 6 hours • Cooker capacity 5.5 litres

1 kg (2 lb 3 oz) piece chuck steak, cut into 6 steaks
1 onion, chopped
1 cup beef stock
4 tablespoons Worcestershire sauce
1 tablespoon minced garlic
3 teaspoons Dijon mustard
1½ cups sliced mushrooms
3 tablespoons cornflour (cornstarch)
½ cup cream

1. Place the steaks into the slow cooker. Mix the onion, stock, Worcestershire sauce, garlic and mustard together and pour over the steaks.
2. Cover and cook on LOW for 3 hours. Add the mushrooms and cook for a further 3 hours.
3. Transfer steaks to a plate and cover with foil.
4. Mix the cornflour and 2 tablespoons water in a small bowl until smooth. Stir into the sauce to thicken.
5. Stir in the cream and return steaks to the sauce to heat through.

Lynda Eagleson

Slow Cooked Beef & Red Wine Stew

Cheap and cheerful!

Serves 6 • Preparation 15 mins • Cook 8 hours • Cooker capacity 3.5 litres

1 kg (2 lb 3 oz) stewing steak, diced
1 red capsicum (pepper), chopped
1 tomato, chopped
1 cup red wine
½ cup beef stock
1 tablespoon tomato paste (concentrated puree)
1 teaspoon dried thyme
1 teaspoon dried rosemary
1 tablespoon cornflour (cornstarch)
Mashed potato, to serve

1. Combine the beef, vegetables, red wine, stock, tomato paste and herbs in the slow cooker.
2. Cover and cook on LOW for 8 hours.
3. Mix the cornflour and 1 tablespoon water in a small bowl until smooth. Stir into the sauce to thicken.
4. Serve with mashed potatoes

NOTE: If you have leftovers, this is great as a filling for a pie.

Corrina Conlan

Slow Cooker Ox Tongue Casserole

My grandma was a farmer's wife, and as such, she tended to use all of the animal after butchering it. One of the things she would use is the tongue. While this isn't her recipe, I did grow up with a taste for tongue! This is a low cost, tender and flavourful cut of meat that I get from our butcher.

Serves 4 • Preparation 20 mins • Cook 6–8 hours • Cooker capacity 5.5 litres

Spray oil
2–3 ox tongue tips, diced
1 onion, diced
2 carrots, diced
3 celery sticks, sliced
50 g (1 ¾ oz) bacon, chopped
1 cup red wine
140 g (5 oz) can or tub tomato paste
1 beef stock cube, crumbled
½ teaspoon garlic powder
½ teaspoon dried thyme
2 bay leaves
Mashed potato or steamed rice, to serve

1. Spray the inside of the slow cooker with oil. Add the ox tongue, onion, carrots, celery and bacon.
2. Whisk together the wine, tomato paste, stock cube, garlic powder and thyme. Season with salt and pepper. Pour into the slow cooker and stir through. Add the bay leaves.
3. Cover and cook on LOW for 6–8 hours.
4. Serve with mashed potato or steamed rice.

Melissa Hansen

Beef, Chickpea & Coconut Red Curry

This is a budget friendly recipe because it allows you to use a cheaper beef cut, and the chickpeas make it go further. Any leftovers used for lunches the next day.

Serves 6 • Preparation 10 mins • Cook 6 hours • Cooker capacity 5.5 litres

1 kg (2 lb 3 oz) stewing steak, cubed
4 cups beef or vegetable stock
2 onions, sliced
400 g (14 oz) can chickpeas, rinsed and drained
½ cup red curry paste
400 ml (13½ fl oz) can coconut cream
Rice and green beans, to serve

1. Place the beef, stock, onion, chickpeas and curry paste into the slow cooker.
2. Cover and cook on LOW for 5½ hours or until beef is tender.
3. Add coconut cream and cook for a further 30 minutes.
4. Serve with rice and green beans.

NOTE: I like to buy cubed beef and I marinate it with the curry paste the night before.

Mel Crean

Corned Silverside

I randomly decided to try this and it tastes absolutely beautiful. I would recommend this recipe to anyone wanting to try corned silverside in a slow cooker. Enjoy!

Serves 4 (with leftovers) • Preparation 20 mins • Cook 6½ hours • Cooker capacity 5.5 Litres

2 brown onions, halved
2 carrots, thickly sliced
1.5 kg (3 lb 5 oz) piece silverside
8 cups beef stock
¼ cup brown sugar
¼ cup malt vinegar
2½ bay leaves
2 garlic cloves
White sauce and vegetables, to serve

1. Place the onions and carrots into the slow cooker and place the silverside on top. Add the remaining ingredients and 4 cups water.
2. Cover and cook on LOW for 6½ hours.
3. Serve with white sauce and vegetables.

Rebecca Roberts

Steak Bolognese

I wanted to try a new way with bolognese using something other than mince, as I didn't have any at the time. I had some steak, so I made this using what I had in my pantry and everyone in the household loved it.

Serves 4 • Preparation 10 mins • Cook 6–8 hrs • Cooker capacity 5.5 litres

1 kg (2 lb 3 oz) stewing steak, diced
420 g (15 oz) can condensed tomato soup
400 g (14 oz) can diced tomatoes
1 onion, roughly chopped
3–4 heaped tablespoons tomato paste (concentrated puree)
1 teaspoon dried mixed herbs
Pasta or mashed potato, to serve

1. Place all the ingredients into the slow cooker.
2. Cover and cook on LOW for 6–8 hours.
3. Serve with pasta or mashed potato.

Nicole Morris

Beef Cheek & Guinness Stew

Beef cheeks were made for the slow cooker. This winter warmer is a must-try.

Serves 2 • Preparation 10 mins • Cook 4–6 hours • Cooker capacity 5.5 litres

2 carrots, chopped
2 potatoes, chopped
1½ cups peas
1½ cups chopped beans
1 onion, chopped
2 tablespoons plain (all-purpose) flour
1 tablespoon dried thyme
400 g (14 oz) can diced tomatoes
200 ml (7 fl oz) Guinness stout
2 beef cheeks

1. Combine the vegetables, flour and thyme in the slow cooker and toss to combine.
2. Stir in the tomatoes and stout, and add the beef cheeks.
3. Cover and cook on LOW for 4–6 hours or until beef cheeks are very tender.

NOTE: If you want a thicker sauce, remove the lid 30 minutes before serving and increase to HIGH.

Denise Roberts

Nana's Choc Casserole

This isn't really chocolate of course, but the rich, thick gravy does resemble chocolate. When my children were young they thought they were being given meat hidden in a chocolate sauce as a trick! This recipe is now a tradition for family gatherings, especially on cold nights.

Serves 4 • Preparation 15 mins • Cook 4 or 8 hours • Cooker capacity 4 litres

700 g (1 lb 9 oz) stewing steak, cubed
1 tablespoon plain (all-purpose) flour
1 tablespoon brown sugar
1 teaspoon ground cinnamon
½ teaspoon curry powder
½ teaspoon ground ginger
¼ teaspoon ground cloves
39 g (1½ oz) packet oxtail soup mix
800 g (1 lb 12 oz) can diced tomatoes (or 2 tablespoon tomato sauce)

1. Combine the steak, flour, sugar and spices in the slow cooker and toss to coat. Sprinkle the soup mix over, add the tomatoes or the tomato sauce mixed with 2 cups water.
2. Cover and cook on HIGH for 4 hours or LOW for 8 hours. If you are around, stir occasionally.

Rebecca George

Italian Steak & Chorizo

I love steak. I love chorizo. So it totally made sense to me to fuse these two big hitters together into one delicious meal. This slow cooked steak meal goes perfectly with any side, but a nice tossed salad is a great combination. Enjoy!

Serves 4 • Preparation 15 mins • Cook 4 hours • Cooker capacity 5 litres

700 g (1 lb 9 oz) blade steak
130 g (4½ oz) chorizo sausage, sliced
100 g (3½ oz) mushrooms, sliced
1 tablespoon chopped fresh basil
1 teaspoon chopped fresh oregano
1 teaspoon chopped fresh thyme
1 teaspoon cracked black pepper
100 g (3½ oz) capsicum (pepper), diced

1. Layer the ingredients into the slow cooker bowl in the order listed, except the capsicum.
2. Cover and cook on HIGH for 3½ hours. Add the capsicum and cook for a further 30 minutes.

NOTE: Remove the steak using a flat lifter. Omit the capsicum if desired. I used it as an extra flavour booster.

Simon Christie

Osso Bucco on a Budget

My local butcher had osso bucco on offer and I bought around 6 pieces, not really having any idea what it was. Now it's a family favourite and one of the recipes I really enjoy doing in the slow cooker.

Serves 6 • Preparation 10 mins • Cook 6 hours • Cooker capacity 6 litres

2 large onions, thinly sliced
2 large carrots, thinly sliced
1 cup peas
6 pieces osso bucco
¼ cup soy sauce
¼ cup Worcestershire sauce
¼ cup BBQ sauce

1. Place the onions, carrots and peas in the bottom of the slow cooker. Add the osso bucco, in a single layer if possible.
2. Add the remaining ingredients and 1 cup water. Cook on HIGH for 6–8 hours.

NOTE: I also add any sauce that will soon be finished, rinsing the bottle with the 1 cup of water.

Tania Farr

1-2-3 Roast Beef

This recipe was inspired by Grace Macdonald, a group member who did a similar recipe with pork – thanks Grace! I had beef to use up one day and easily adapted Grace's recipe. It was amazing! It's now become a regular in our house. It's as easy as 1–2–3! Who doesn't love easy?

Serves 6 • Preparation 5 mins • Cook 6–8 hours • Cooker capacity 6 litres

1 kg (2 lb 3 oz) rolled rib beef roast (or larger)
1½ tablespoons gravy powder of your choice (I use traditional)
Roast vegetables, to serve

1. Place the beef into the slow cooker and sprinkle with gravy powder. Pour ½ cup warm water over the roast.
2. Cover and cook on LOW for 6 hours, or longer if you are using a larger roast.
3. Slice and serve with the gravy and roast vegetables.

Paulene Christie

Simple Saucy Shredded Beef

A versatile, simple and saucy shredded beef that my nine year old nephew loves making and requests often. This is also a perfect pie filling.

Serves 8 • Preparation 15 mins • Cook 9–10 hours • Cooker capacity 5.5 litres

1 cup diced carrot
2 cups finely diced celery
2 spring onions (scallions), sliced
1 tablespoon fresh thyme leaves (or ¾ teaspoon dried)
2 teaspoons chopped fresh rosemary (or ½ teaspoon dried)
3 bay leaves
1.5 kg (3 lb 5 oz) piece beef topside
1½ cups vegetable stock
1–2 cups gravy, made from gravy powder according to packet directions
Bread rolls, to serve

1. Combine the vegetables and herbs in the slow cooker and sit the beef on top. Pour in the stock.
2. Cover and cook on LOW for 9–10 hours, until the beef is tender enough to pull apart.
3. Remove the bay leaves and use 2 forks to shred the meat. Stir to combine with the vegetables.
4. Add the gravy and stir through, or serve meat mixture on bread rolls and drizzle with gravy.

NOTE: Use only the green part of the spring onions if following a FODMAP diet.

Felicity Barnett and Alexander Cox

Lazy Budget Pies

I made 12 of these for under $15! I didn't make them from a recipe – I just grabbed whatever veggies I had left in the fridge and bought discounted veggies from the shop. The most expensive thing was the pastry, which I'm sure you could make to lower your cost even more. I froze these pies individually for our lunches. Much cheaper than a shop pie and hopefully nicer.

Makes 12 individual pies • Preparation 20 mins • Cook 4 or 6 hours + 20 mins baking • Cooker capacity 5.5 litres

- 1 kg (2 lb 3 oz) stewing steak, chopped
- ½ bunch celery, chopped
- 400 g (14 oz) can corn kernels, drained
- 250 g (9 oz) mushrooms, sliced
- 2 carrots, chopped
- ½ onion, chopped
- 3 garlic cloves, minced
- 2 tablespoons gravy powder
- 2 tablespoons stock powder
- Few sprigs fresh rosemary
- 2 tablespoons cornflour (cornstarch)
- 6 sheets frozen puff pastry, thawed
- Lightly beaten egg or melted butter, to brush
- Sesame seeds, to sprinkle

1. Combine the beef, celery, corn, mushrooms, carrots, onion, garlic, gravy and stock powders, and rosemary in the slow cooker. Add enough water to just cover.
2. Cover and cook on HIGH for 4 hours or on LOW for 6 hours.
3. Mix the cornflour and 2 tablespoons water in a small bowl until smooth. Stir into the sauce to thicken. Transfer to a large bowl, season with salt and pepper and cool completely.
4. Pre-heat the oven to 180°C (350°F/Gas 4). Cut pastry into quarters and use half the pieces to line twelve 1 cup capacity pie tins. Fill with meat mixture and top with remaining pastry, pressing the edges to seal. Brush with egg or melted butter and sprinkle with sesame seeds.
5. Cook for 20 minutes or until golden brown.

NOTE: Depending on what's on sale you can always replace the steak with chicken, and use curry powder instead of gravy for a yummy curried chicken and vegetable pie. If using chicken, reduce the cooking time to 3 hours on HIGH or 5 hours on LOW.

Kelly Brereton

Ballsy Braised Beef

This is a great winter dish, and it freezes beautifully. It's very versatile, but I love to just eat it on buttered toast.

Serves 8 • Preparation 10 mins • Cook 6–8 hours • Cooker capacity 6 litres

1 large onion, diced
2 carrots, diced
1–2 celery stalks, diced
1 red or green chilli, deseeded and finely chopped (optional)
1 tablespoon olive oil
1.2 kg (3 lb 5 oz) gravy beef
400 g (14 oz) can diced tomatoes
1 cup beef stock
Mashed potato, or pasta and crusty bread, to serve

1. Combine the onion, carrot, celery and chilli (if using) in a slow cooker.
2. Heat the oil in a frying pan over medium-high heat and cook the beef for a couple of minutes each side, until browned. Add to the slow cooker.
3. Pour the tomatoes and stock over, and season with salt and pepper.
4. Cover and cook on LOW for 6–8 hours, until the meat pulls apart with a fork.
5. Discard any fat or sinew from the meat, and serve with mashed potato or pasta and bread.

NOTE: You can skip the browning step if you like, but it adds good flavour to the meat.

Tennille Langley

Smoky BBQ & Onion Pulled Beef

When we go on holidays we take our trusty slow cooker with us. During one recent holiday, we wanted a recipe for a simple meal we could leave all day to do its own thing in the slow cooker. We wanted to be able to come home after a long day at the theme parks and find dinner all ready. This was perfect! On holidays we serve it straight onto crusty bread rolls for an extra easy meal. When we cook this at home with more time to spare it's lovely on mashed sweet potato or potato.

Serves 6 • Preparation 5 mins • Cook 5 hours • Cooker capacity 5 litres

1.5 kg (3 lb 5 oz) topside beef roast
1 large brown onion, thinly sliced
1 cup BBQ sauce/marinade/baste

1. Place the beef into the slow cooker. Spread the onion on top, then pour the sauce over.
2. Cover and cook on HIGH for 5 hours.
3. Use two forks to shred the meat.

NOTE: I use McCormick Vintage Smokehouse Grill Mate BBQ Sauce/Marinade/Baste.

Paulene Christie

Beef Korma

We love curries and I decided to attempt one without a packet mix or jar of sauce. This turned out really well!

Serves 4–6 • Preparation 15 minutes • Cook 5 hours • Cooker capacity 3.5 litres

2 onions, finely diced
4 garlic cloves, minced
2.5 cm (1 inch) piece fresh ginger, finely grated
1 teaspoon oil
2 tablespoons ground almonds
1 tablespoon garam masala
1 teaspoon red curry paste (optional)
1 teaspoon salt
1 teaspoon paprika
1 cup beef stock
3 tablespoons tomato paste
1.5 kg (3 lb 5 oz) blade steak, cut into 2.5 cm (1 inch) cubes
⅔ cup plain natural yoghurt
2 tablespoons cornflour (cornstarch)

1. Combine the onions, garlic, ginger and oil in a frying pan on low heat and cook for about 5 minutes, until onions are soft and translucent.
2. Add the ground almonds, garam masala, red curry paste (if using), salt and paprika. Cook for 2 minutes.
3. Stir in the stock and tomato paste, and cook for 2 minutes. Transfer the mixture to the slow cooker and stir in the beef.
4. Cover and cook on HIGH for 1 hour, then reduce to LOW and cook for 4 hours.
5. Approximately 20 minutes before the end of the cooking time mix the yoghurt and cornflour until smooth and stir into the beef mixture.

NOTE: Cook on LOW for 6 hours, if you prefer. To make a chicken version, use chicken thighs. Cook on HIGH for 1 hour, then LOW for 3 hours.

Nikki Willis

Pepper Steak

I've always like pepper steak from the Chinese take-away, but with a family of five these types of purchases can really put a dent in the budget. This recipe makes enough to feed our family, for a fraction of the cost of buying the several containers of take-away equivalent. Bulk up the meal with sides of rice, noodles or couscous to make your budget go even further.

Serves 4 • Preparation 15 mins • Cook 2 hours • Cooker capacity 5 litres

800 g (1 lb 12 oz) rump steak, sliced into thin strips
1 tablespoon plain (all-purpose) flour
2 teaspoons olive oil
2 cups (loosely packed) very fine strips or shreds of carrot
1 small red capsicum (pepper), cut into strips
¼ cup reduced-salt soy sauce
1 tablespoon white wine vinegar
1 tablespoon minced garlic
2 teaspoons minced ginger
1 teaspoon freshly cracked black pepper
20 snow peas, trimmed, halved diagonally
Couscous, to serve, if desired

1. Place the beef strips in a plastic freezer bag with the flour. Shake to coat.
2. Heat the oil in a searing slow cooker (or in a frying pan on the stove) and sear the beef until brown.
3. Combine the beef, carrot and capsicum in the slow cooker. Mix the soy sauce, vinegar, garlic, ginger and pepper, and pour over.
4. Cover and cook on HIGH for 1½ hours. Add the snow peas and cook for a further 30 minutes.
5. Serve with couscous, if desired.

Paulene Christie

CHICKEN

Paprika Chicken

While a lot of our chicken recipes are cooked in sauces of some kind, this is a great alternative for anyone wanting just simple seasoned chicken. You can replace the drumsticks with any cut of chicken, on or off the bone. Wings would be even more budget friendly. Great served with salad, chips or vegetables.

Serves 4 • Preparation 10 mins • Cook 4½ hours • Cooker capacity 5 litres

8 chicken drumsticks
1 tablespoon finely chopped fresh parsley
2 teaspoons paprika
4 garlic cloves, minced
1 teaspoon garlic salt
1 teaspoon olive oil
Salad, chips or vegetables, to serve

1. Place the chicken drumsticks into the slow cooker. Combine the remaining ingredients and scatter over the chicken.
2. Using a large plastic or wooden spoon, mix the drumsticks around so they become coated.
3. Cover and cook on LOW for 4½ hours.

NOTE: There is no need to brown the chicken first, but you can if you prefer to.

Paulene Christie

Creamy Garlic & Sweet Chilli Chicken Pasta

As I looked through recipes for the perfect pasta dish, I decided to create my own. Using basic ingredients I usually have in the fridge and cupboard, this dish is simple yet delicious.

Serves 4 • Preparation 10 mins • Cook 3 hours • Cooker capacity 3.5 litres

500 g (1 lb 2 oz) chicken breast fillets, diced
1 onion, diced
1 red capsicum (pepper), sliced
½ cup sweet chilli sauce
2 garlic cloves, minced
300 ml (10 fl oz) cooking cream
½ cup grated parmesan
Penne pasta, to serve

1. Combine the chicken, onion, capsicum, sweet chilli sauce and garlic in the slow cooker.
2. Cover and cook on HIGH for 2 hours.
3. Stir in the cream and parmesan. Cook for a further 1 hour.
4. Stir through the cooked pasta and serve.

Jenny Krahe

Slow Cooker Mac 'n' Cheese Chicken

After trying a few varieties of mac 'n' cheese I thought something was absent from the meal. That got me thinking in man terms – protein! So I added chicken and this is the result. A one-pot, simple, filling meal for all the family.

Serves 6 • Preparation 10 mins • Cook 3 hours • Cooker capacity 5 litres

3 chicken thigh fillets, diced
500 g (1 lb 2 oz) block cheddar, roughly cut into 8 pieces
1 tablespoon wholegrain mustard
1 tablespoon minced garlic
500 g (1 lb 2 oz) uncooked macaroni

1. Place the chicken into the slow cooker. Add the cheese, mustard, garlic and 4 cups water, then stir in the macaroni.
2. Cover and cook on HIGH for 3 hours, stirring occasionally, until the macaroni is tender.

Simon Christie

Cheesy Salami Chicken

What's not to love about these three ingredients ... especially when they are all together! Jarlsberg is a lovely melting cheese that's perfect for this dish, but mozzarella would work too if you prefer that. We keep the salami mild for our children's tastebuds but if you like heat by all means you could change yours to a hot salami. Our children love this recipe and ask for it often.

Serves 5 • Preparation 5 mins • Cook 4 hours • Cooker capacity 5 litres

5 chicken thigh cutlets (bone in), or chicken pieces of your choice
5 slices mild salami
5 slices Jarlsberg cheese

1. Place the chicken cutlets into the slow cooker.
2. Cover and cook on HIGH for 3 hours.
3. Carefully remove the chicken with a slotted spoon and set aside. Drain all the liquid from the slow cooker, then return the chicken.
4. Lay one slice of salami on top of each chicken piece, then place a slice of Jarlsberg on top (if you have excess cheese you can double it over).
5. Cover, putting a tea towel (dish towel) under the lid, and cook on LOW for 1 hour.

NOTE: You can adapt this recipe to however many serves you need.

Paulene Christie

BBQ Plum Chicken

This recipe was inspired by a similar sauce I use with the Asian Meatballs recipe from *Slow Cooker Central* book 1 which I absolutely love! Because I eat a lot of chicken I decided to try the flavours together and I wasn't disappointed. We like to serve ours with creamy mashed potato and vegetables so we can drizzle the sauce over the mash.

Serves 5 • Preparation 5 mins • Cook 5 hours • Cooker capacity 6 litres

10 chicken drumsticks
½ cup BBQ sauce
¼ cup plum sauce
2 tablespoons hoisin sauce
2 garlic cloves, minced
Mashed potato and steamed vegetables, to serve

1. Place the chicken into the slow cooker. Combine all the other ingredients and pour over the chicken.
2. Cover and cook on low for 5 hours.
3. Serve with mashed potato and steamed vegetables.

NOTE: I thicken the sauce by mixing 1 tablespoon cornflour with 1 tablespoon water until smooth. Stir into the sauce 10 minutes before serving.

Paulene Christie

Homestyle Satay Wings

This is a cheap yet satisfying alternative to buying pre-marinated or flavoured wings from your local deli. This is a dish for those who like to know exactly what goes into their cooking. Personally I was impressed with the final flavours in this, and have always enjoyed rave reviews from my family too.

Serves 4–6 • Preparation 15 mins • Cook 4 hours • Cooker capacity: 5 litres

1 kg (2 lb 3 oz) chicken wings, tips removed, halved at the joint
165 ml (5½ fl oz) can coconut milk
½ cup chicken stock
¼ cup peanut butter
2 tablespoons reduced-salt soy sauce
2 teaspoons cornflour (cornstarch)
2 teaspoons minced garlic
2 teaspoons minced ginger
1 teaspoon brown sugar

1. Place the wings into the slow cooker. Mix the remaining ingredients in a bowl, ensuring the peanut butter is thoroughly blended in. Pour over the wings.
2. Cover and cook on LOW for 2½ hours. Remove excess oils by skimming the surface with a dessert spoon.
3. Cover, putting a tea towel (dish towel) under the lid, and cook for a further 1½ hours.

Simon Christie

One Pot Chicken Dinner

Knowing we were going to be late home I wanted a simple, ready-to-serve meal waiting for us. This has since become a go-to meal. My daughter, who normally eats potatoes only if they have been mashed, loves the potatoes and describes them as "like creamy mashed potato without having to mash them".

Serves 4–6 • Preparation 15 mins • Cook 6–7 hours • Cooker capacity 5.5 litres

500 g (1 lb 2 oz) small potatoes, quartered
2 carrots, cut into batons
1 leek, sliced
3 garlic cloves
2 teaspoons thyme leaves
2 bay leaves
½ cup cream
2 tablespoons cornflour (cornstarch)
1 cup chicken stock
1 kg (2 lb 3 oz) chicken pieces (any cut you like)
Pinch cracked pepper
100 g (3½ oz) fresh green beans

1. Place the potatoes, carrots, leek, garlic, thyme and bay leaves into the slow cooker. Stir the cream and cornflour together until smooth. Pour over the vegetables, along with the stock.
2. Place the chicken pieces on top of the vegetables and sprinkle with the pepper.
3. Cover and cook on LOW for 6–7 hours.
4. Add the beans for the last hour of cooking, or add earlier if you are not going to be around. Remove the bay leaves and serve.

NOTE: I have used breast fillets, thighs, cutlets and marylands with success. Garlic can be left whole, sliced or crushed – whatever you prefer. Lactose-free cream can be used for a lactose-free version, or it can be made dairy-free by omitting the cream and adding an extra ¼ cup stock.

Felicity Barnett

Tropical BBQ Chicken

My kids love honey BBQ chicken. Adding the pineapple gives it a nice tang.

Serves 4 • Preparation 5 mins • Cook 6 hours • Cooker capacity 6 litres

1 kg (2 lb 3 oz) chicken drumsticks
440 g (15½ oz) can crushed pineapple, drained
⅔ cup BBQ sauce
2 tablespoons honey
1 tablespoon golden syrup
Vegetables and mashed potato, pasta or rice, to serve

1. Place the chicken drumsticks in the slow cooker in a single layer. Pour the drained pineapple over the drumsticks.
2. Combine the BBQ sauce, honey and golden syrup then pour over the chicken and pineapple.
3. Cover and cook on LOW for 6 hours.
4. Serve with vegetables and mashed potato, pasta or rice.

Narelle Youngs

Spring Vegetable Chicken

This recipe came to me while trying to put something together extremely quickly during a busy morning, in preparation for a busy evening. It turned out to be quite delicious. Everyone enjoyed it.

Serves 4 • Preparation 10 mins • Cook 6–8 hours • Cooker capacity 6 litres

400 g (14 oz) can diced tomatoes
30 g (1 oz) packet spring vegetable soup mix
1 tablespoon Worcestershire sauce
8 chicken drumsticks
400 g (14 oz) sweet potato, chopped
200 g (7 oz) green beans, chopped
2 zucchini, chopped
100 g (3½ oz) mushrooms, halved
1 tablespoon cornflour (cornstarch)
Couscous, to serve

1. Place the tomatoes, soup mix, Worcestershire sauce and 1½ cups water into the slow cooker, and stir to combine. Add the chicken and vegetables and mix well.
2. Cover and cook on LOW for 6–8 hours.
3. Remove the chicken and set aside. Mix the cornflour and 1 tablespoon water in a small bowl until smooth. Stir into the sauce to thicken. Return the chicken to heat through.
4. Serve with couscous.

NOTE: Cook on HIGH for 3–4 hours if you prefer. You can use any vegetables you have on hand. Couscous is very quick to prepare, but you could serve rice or mash if you like.

Sharon Ramsden

Mummabear's Marinated Chicken

I wanted to try a marinade for chicken as I have never done one before, so I used these simple ingredients and something wonderful happened. It's certainly a family favourite.

Serves 6 • Preparation 10 mins • Cook 4–6 hours • Cooker capacity 6 litres

1 kg (2 lb 3 oz) chicken breast fillets
1 cup BBQ sauce
5 garlic cloves, minced
Rice or stir-fried vegetables, to serve

1. Cut the chicken into bite-sized chunks or strips and place into the slow cooker.
2. Stir in the BBQ sauce and garlic.
3. Cover and cook on LOW for 4–6 hours.
4. Serve with rice or stir-fried vegetables.

Kara Johnson

Cheesy Mexican Chilli Mac

I love this recipe because it is easy, cheap and versatile, and it feeds an army! You can use any meat, or no meat at all – just change the type of stock you are using. You can leave out the taco mix if your kids don't like spice – just add some Italian herbs instead. Any dry pasta can be used in place of macaroni.

Serves 8–10 • Preparation 20 mins • Cook 6–6½ hours • Cooker capacity 6 litres

500 g (1 lb 2 oz) chicken breast fillets
2 x 400 g (14 oz) cans diced tomato
2 cups chicken stock
½ onion, diced
30 g (1 oz) packet taco seasoning mix
1 tablespoon minced garlic
400 g (14 oz) can black beans, rinsed and drained
1½ cups combined grated carrot and zucchini
3 cups macaroni
2 cups grated tasty cheese
Sour cream, to serve

1. Combine the chicken, tomato, stock, onion, taco seasoning and garlic in the slow cooker.
2. Cover and cook on LOW for 5 hours.
3. Remove the chicken and shred using tongs or two forks. Return to the slow cooker with the beans and vegetables. Cook for 30 minutes.
4. Stir in the macaroni and cheese, and cook for a further 30–60 minutes, or until the pasta is cooked and the cheese has melted. Serve with sour cream.

NOTE: Use kidney beans or lentils instead of black beans, if you prefer. The grated veggies can be replaced with frozen chopped veggies.

Shannen Edge

Hickory BBQ Chicken

It really doesn't get any easier than this: a simple pulled chicken that is a great budget option. It goes a long way so it's great to add to the food table at your next big party. Your guests can even serve themselves straight from the slow cooker. The sauce aisle of your supermarket is packed with many different flavour options you can use if you don't like Hickory BBQ, so choose whatever you like. You can even choose reduced-salt or low-sugar sauces if you want to cut the salt and calories from your diet.

Serves 6 • Preparation 5 mins • Cook 4 hours • Cooker capacity 5 litres

1 kg (2 lb 3 oz) chicken thigh fillets
250 ml (9 fl oz) bottle Hickory BBQ Sauce
Bread rolls, salad and grated tasty cheese, to serve

1. Place the whole chicken fillets into the slow cooker and pour the sauce over.
2. Cover and cook on LOW for 4 hours.
3. Use two forks to pull apart and shred the chicken, which will then soak up all the excess sauce.

Serve on rolls with salad and cheese for easy 'burgers'.

NOTE: You can easily change the flavour by using satay, BBQ plum or honey soy sauce.

Paulene Christie

Pulled Balsamic Chicken

This recipe is very easy and very tasty. The chicken can be served on wraps with coleslaw, or you can use it in tacos and burritos, or on sandwiches.

Serves 8 • Preparation 5 mins • Cook 5 hours • Cooker capacity 5.5 litres

1 kg (2 lb 3 oz) chicken thigh or breast fillets
Paprika, to taste
¾ cup balsamic vinegar
⅓ cup brown sugar
2 teaspoons minced garlic

1. Season the chicken well with paprika, salt and pepper and place into the slow cooker.
2. Mix the vinegar, sugar and garlic and pour over the chicken.
3. Cover and cook on LOW for 5 hours.
4. Take chicken out of the slow cooker and use 2 forks to shred and pull apart. Put back into the cooking liquid and mix well. Serve as desired.

NOTE: I prefer chicken thigh fillets as they don't dry out as much.

Lynda Eagleson

Chicken & Leek Pie

This is a family favourite recipe I had been cooking on the stovetop for years. I decided to give it a try in the slow cooker and it turned out to be absolutely delicious! I always serve mine with a salad, some veggies or chips – anything you like really!

Serves 4–6 • Preparation 15 mins • Cook 4 hours + 30 mins baking • Cooker capacity 6 litres

5 chicken thigh fillets, roughly chopped
1 cup chicken stock
1 onion, diced
1 leek, halved lengthways then cut into 1 cm (½ inch) slices
1 tablespoon wholegrain mustard
Sprinkle dried tarragon
1 tablespoon cornflour (cornstarch)
¼–½ cup cream (to your taste)
2 sheets puff pastry
1 egg, lightly beaten (optional)

1. Combine the chicken, stock, onion, leek, mustard and tarragon in the slow cooker.
2. Cover and cook on HIGH for 3½ hours.
3. Mix the cornflour and 1 tablespoon water in a small bowl until smooth. Stir into the sauce, along with the cream. Cover and cook for a further 30 minutes, until thickened.
4. Pre-heat the oven to 180°C (350°F/Gas 4). Line a pie dish with 1 sheet puff pastry. Spoon the filling in, then cover with remaining pastry. Seal the edges and brush with egg (if using). Bake for 30 minutes or until pastry is crisp and golden.

Katrina Jenner

Taco Chicken

I love chicken. If I could only eat one type of meat for the rest of my life chicken would be it, so I'm always trying to come up with new ways to cook it. Tasty taco seasoning is a great way to add maximum flavour with minimal effort and cost. The first time I tried to cook this, I had to throw it out after a power outage for several hours left my slow cooker turned off! I was determined to try again, and it was totally worth it in the end.

Serves 6 • Preparation 15 mins • Cook 4 hours • Cooker capacity 5 litres

2 kg (4 lb 6 oz) whole chicken
35 g (1 oz) packet taco seasoning mix
Salad and sour cream (optional), to serve

1. Place the chicken into the slow cooker, breast side down. Make 8–10 piercings over the chicken with a sharp knife tip.
2. Sprinkle ⅔ of the taco seasoning over the chicken. Rub into the chicken, especially into the cuts. Sprinkle with remaining taco seasoning.
3. Cover and cook on AUTO for 4 hours. Spoon some of the cooking juices over the chicken 2–3 times during cooking.
4. Serve with salad and a dollop of sour cream (if using).

NOTE: If you don't have an AUTO setting on your slow cooker, cook on LOW for 5 hours. Cooking the chicken with the breast down makes for a moist chicken breast when served. I use two egg flips to get under each end of the chicken to lift it out when cooked – you could cook it on a trivet or in a chicken sling if you prefer.

Paulene Christie

Pesto Chicken

This is an absolute family favourite. We have this dish at least once per fortnight and everyone's plates are clean at the end of the meal. The flavours are very complementary. Pesto chicken is great served with creamy mashed potato, and salad or steamed vegetables.

Serves 4 • Preparation 10 mins • Cook 4–5 hours • Cooker capacity 6 litres

4 chicken breast fillets
2 tablespoons dried parsley flakes
1 teaspoon dried dill
1 teaspoon dried basil
1 teaspoon garlic powder
1 teaspoon onion powder
1 teaspoon cracked black pepper
1 cup basil pesto

1. Place the chicken into the slow cooker.
2. Combine the parsley, dill, basil, garlic powder, onion powder and pepper in a small bowl and mix well. Sprinkle evenly over the chicken.
3. Stir the pesto with ½ cup water until combined. Pour over the chicken to coat.
4. Cover and cook on LOW for 4–5 hours.

NOTE: I have also made this dish using tenderloins, and reducing the cooking time to 3–4 hours.

Lisa Peacock

Peri Peri Chicken

I'd always enjoyed peri peri flavours but I'd never tried to cook the chicken myself before this recipe. I researched the various flavours that make up the traditional tastes and set about converting to a slow cooker-friendly recipe with great results. Remember to allow time for the chicken to marinate overnight for a good depth of flavour. It is quite a spicy dish so it may not be well received by little people at your table but it is certainly one the more mature taste buds can enjoy.

Serves 6 • Preparation 20 mins + marinating • Cook 4 hours • Cooker capacity 5 litres

1 kg (2 lb 3 oz) chicken thigh or breast fillets
1 tablespoon olive oil
1 tablespoon chopped dried chilli (or 2 tablespoons chopped fresh chilli)
1 tablespoon chopped fresh parsley
1 tablespoon paprika
4 garlic cloves, minced
2 teaspoons minced ginger
Juice of 1 lemon
1 teaspoon dried oregano
1 teaspoon salt
½ teaspoon cracked black pepper

1. Lay the chicken fillets in a non-metal tray or container with a lid. Combine all the other ingredients to make a marinade.
2. Pour the marinade over the chicken. Cover and marinate in the fridge overnight, or at least for a few hours.
3. Gently transfer the chicken to the slow cooker, trying to keep the marinade in place.
4. Cover and cook on LOW for 4 hours.

Paulene Christie

Chicken Casserole

When I was a kid growing up on a farm this was my favourite meal, and it still is. I used to help my mum make this – another delicious family recipe passed down through the years. My favourite part of this recipe is eating it with 2-minute noodles, but that is optional as not everyone likes noodles.

Serves 4 • Preparation 10 mins • Cook 4–6 hours • Cooker capacity 6 litres

2 chicken breast fillets, chopped
1 large onion, chopped
¼ cabbage, chopped
2 potatoes, chopped
500 g (1 lb 2 oz) mixed frozen vegetables
50 g (1 ¾ oz) packet chicken noodle soup mix
1 teaspoon salt
2-minute noodles, to serve

1. Combine the chicken, onion, cabbage and potatoes in the slow cooker. Add the mixed vegetables, soup mix, salt and 4–5 cups water. Stir to combine.
2. Cover and cook on HIGH for 4–6 hours. Check after about 30 minutes. If the dish is looking watery, add a little cornflour to thicken.
3. Serve with 2-minute noodles.

Trinity Simmons

My (Easy) Thai Chicken Curry

I adapted this recipe from several types of Thai chicken recipes. It's suitable for a low budget family meal and freezes well too.

Serves 4 • Preparation 20 mins • Cook 6 hours • Cooker capacity 3.5 or 6 litres

1 tablespoon olive oil
1 onion, sliced
2–3 tablespoons green curry paste
3 teaspoons minced garlic
Red chilli flakes, to taste
1 kg (2 lb 3 oz) chicken thigh fillets
2 cups chicken stock
400 ml (13½ fl oz) can coconut milk
Snow peas or frozen vegetables of your choice
Lime juice, to taste
1–2 teaspoons sugar, to taste (optional)
Rice or noodles, to serve

1. Heat the olive oil in a frying pan over medium heat. Cook the onion for about 3 minutes, until soft. Add the curry paste, garlic and chilli flakes. Cook, stirring, for 1 minute. Place into the slow cooker.
2. Add the chicken, stock, coconut milk and vegetables to the cooker and stir to combine.
3. Cover and cook on LOW for 5 hours. Remove the lid, increase to HIGH and cook for 1 more hour, to reduce and thicken the sauce.
4. Season with lime juice and sugar (if using), to taste. Serve with rice or noodles.

NOTE: Stir in 1 tablespoon cornflour (cornstarch) mixed with 1 tablespoon water at the end if it's not the thickness you like.

Robyn Clark

Honey Soy Chicken

This is easy to make and yummy to eat, and both adults and kids like it!

Serves 5 • Preparation 15 mins • Cook 4 hours • Cooker capacity 6 litres

1 tablespoon vegetable oil
10 chicken thigh fillets
175 g (6 oz) honey
175 ml (6 fl oz) light soy sauce
¼ cup tomato sauce (ketchup)
2 garlic cloves, minced
1 tablespoon minced fresh ginger
440 g (15½ oz) can pineapple pieces, drained, juice reserved
2 tablespoons cornflour (cornstarch)
Rice and/or vegetables, to serve

1. Heat the oil in a frying pan over medium heat, and brown the chicken on all sides.
2. Pour the honey, soy sauce, tomato sauce, garlic, ginger and reserved pineapple juice into a slow cooker and mix well. Place the chicken into the slow cooker and turn to coat with mixture.
3. Cover and cook on HIGH for 4 hours. Stir in the pineapple for the final 20 minutes of cooking.
4. Mix the cornflour and ⅓ cup water in a small bowl. Remove thighs from slow cooker. Blend the cornflour mixture into the sauce in the slow cooker to thicken.
5. Serve the chicken with rice and/or vegetables, with the sauce poured over the top.

Lyn Collins

Easy Creamy Chicken Curry

A very versatile curry, made with ease, yet full of flavour. Add as much veg as you like and add more curry for extra bang!

Serves 6–8 • Preparation 10 mins • Cook 6 hours • Cooker capacity 3 litres

1 kg (2 lb 3 oz) chicken thigh fillets, diced
1 chicken stock cube
45 g (1½ oz) packet chicken noodle soup mix
2–3 tablespoons curry powder (I use 2½)
420 g (15 oz) can condensed cream of chicken soup
300 ml (10½ fl oz) light cooking cream
165 ml (5½ fl oz) can coconut milk
2 teaspoons cornflour (cornstarch)
2 cups frozen mixed vegetables (optional)
Rice, pasta or mashed potato, to serve

1. Place the chicken into the slow cooker. Crumble the stock cube over, then sprinkle with the chicken noodle soup mix and curry powder.
2. In a bowl, combine the chicken soup, cooking cream, coconut milk and cornflour. Mix to combine, then pour over the chicken.
3. Cover and cook on LOW for 6 hours, adding the vegetables for the last hour (if using).
4. Serve with rice, pasta or mashed potato.

Sharon King

Cheat's Chicken Burritos

This recipe came about after I'd had a long, exhausting day out with the family. It was the day before I was due to go grocery shopping and all I could find were some staple items in the pantry, some chicken sausages in the freezer and a chilli in the bottom of the crisper, looking a little worse for wear. After a bit of experimenting, I created this dish. My family love it because it's tasty, and I love it because it's speedy to prep.

Makes 8 • Preparation 10 mins • Cook 2–3 hours • Cooker capacity 7 litres

800 g (1 lb 12 oz) can diced tomatoes
30 g (1 oz) packet taco seasoning mix
420 g (15 oz) can red kidney beans, rinsed, drained and coarsely mashed
1 long red chilli, deseeded and finely chopped
8 tortillas
8 good-quality chicken sausages
1 cup grated tasty cheese
Salad, to serve

1. Combine the diced tomatoes, red kidney beans, taco seasoning and chilli in a large bowl. Mix with a metal spoon until well combined.
2. Take one of the tortillas and lay it on a flat surface. Spread 3 tablespoonfuls of the tomato mixture over the entire surface of the tortilla. Lay one sausage along the outer edge of the tortilla and roll up tightly so that the sausage is encased in the centre. Repeat with remaining sausages and tortillas, reserving leftover tomato mixture.
3. Spread half the reserved tomato mixture over the base of the slow cooker. Place the burritos side by side, seam side down, on top of the tomato mixture.
4. Pour the remaining tomato mixture over the top of the burritos and sprinkle the grated cheese evenly over the top.
5. Cover, putting a tea towel (dish towel) under the lid, and cook on HIGH for 2–3 hours. Serve with salad.

Alanna Williams

Honey Balsamic Chicken

I use thigh cutlets for this recipe but other more budget cuts such as wings or drumsticks would be just as good. Don't be afraid to change the chicken to what suits your family best. We like to serve this chicken with salads in summer, or with vegetables in the cooler months.

Serves 5 • Preparation 10 mins • Cook 5 hours • Cooker capacity 6 litres

1.5 kg (3 lb 5 oz) chicken pieces
½ cup balsamic vinegar
½ cup honey
½ cup brown sugar, firmly packed
¼ cup reduced-salt soy sauce
2 teaspoons minced garlic
1 teaspoon minced ginger

1. Place chicken into the slow cooker. Combine all the other ingredients and pour over the chicken.
2. Cover and cook on LOW for 5 hours.

Paulene Christie

Korean Spicy Chicken Stew

This is called dakdoritang in Korea. It is a spicy chicken dish with vegetables.

Serves 4 • Preparation 15 mins • Cook 4 or 6 hours • Cooker capacity 3.5 litres

1 kg (2 lb 3 oz) chicken breast or thigh fillets, cut into small pieces
300 g (10½ oz) potatoes, cut into big chunks
2 carrots, cut into big chunks
½ large onion, cut into big chunks
4–5 garlic cloves
2.5 cm (1 inch) piece ginger, thinly sliced
2 spring onions (scallions), cut into 5 cm (2 inch) lengths
⅓ cup soy sauce
2 tablespoons Korean red chilli powder (gochugaru)
2 tablespoons rice wine
1 tablespoon sugar
1 tablespoon honey
1 tablespoon Korean red chilli paste (gochujang)
1 tablespoon sesame oil
1 teaspoon sesame seeds
Pinch pepper
Rice, to serve

1. Place the chicken and vegetables into the slow cooker. Add the remaining ingredients and stir well.
2. Cover and cook on HIGH for 4 hours or LOW for 6 hours.
3. Serve with a bowl of rice.

Juyea Choi

Sweet Chilli Chicken Noodles

Anyone who knows me knows I love noodles. They're my favourite take-away food, but they're such a dent to the budget when you have a large family that I wanted to make my own version at home – slow cooked of course! This recipe produces enough for the whole family for around what just one serve would cost at a take-away noodle shop. It would also adapt nicely to beef if you prefer that to chicken.

Serves 4 • Preparation 15 mins • Cook 3½ hours • Cooker capacity 5 litres

700 g (1 lb 9 oz) chicken thigh or breast fillets, cut into strips
2 brown onions, cut into thin strips
1 red capsicum (pepper), cut into strips
2 handfuls of snow peas, ends trimmed
1 cup mild sweet chilli sauce
¼ cup honey
1½ tablespoons soy sauce
440 g (15½ oz) shelf-fresh Singapore noodles

1. Place the chicken and onion into the slow cooker.
2. Cover and cook on HIGH for 1 hour, then drain all the liquid.
3. Add the capsicum, snow peas, chilli sauce, honey and soy sauce. Cook for a further 2 hours.
4. Place the noodles in a bowl and pour over 1 cup boiling water. Stand for a couple of minutes to soften and separate the noodles. Drain, and add noodles to the slow cooker. Cook for 30 minutes to heat the noodles through.

NOTE: I use a supermarket brand sweet chilli sauce which isn't overly spicy, so this meal is child friendly for us.

Paulene Christie

Creamy Chicken & Broccoli Casserole

A childhood recipe of my mum's which I adapted for the slow cooker. Note a gluten-free substitute at the bottom.

Serves 4 • Preparation 10 mins • Cook 3½ hours • Cooker capacity 3.5 litres

500 g (1 lb 2 oz) chicken breast fillets, diced
1 head broccoli, chopped
420 g (15 oz) can condensed cream of chicken soup
¼ cup mayonnaise
1 tablespoon lemon juice
1 teaspoon curry powder
½ cup grated tasty cheese
Rice, to serve

1. Combine the chicken and broccoli in the slow cooker. Mix the soup, mayonnaise, lemon juice and curry powder together and pour over the chicken and broccoli. Sprinkle cheese over the top.
2. Cook on HIGH for 2½ hours then reduce to LOW and cook for 1 hour.
3. Serve over rice.

NOTE: For a gluten-free 'condensed chicken soup' combine 3 packets of Basco Creamy Chicken soup with enough water to make up to 375ml.

Jenny Krahe

Creamy Taco Chicken

My family loves chicken and tacos, so I came up with this recipe one night.

Serves 4–6 • Preparation 10 mins • Cook 6 hours • Cooker capacity 5 litres

1 kg (2 lb 3 oz) chicken drumsticks
600 ml (20½ fl oz) cooking cream
30 g (1 oz) packet taco seasoning mix
1 teaspoon minced garlic
Rice and steamed veggies, to serve

1. Place the chicken into the slow cooker.
2. Cover and cook on LOW for 5 hours.
3. Mix the remaining ingredients together and pour over chicken. Season with pepper and cook for 1 hour.

NOTE: You can use any cut of chicken in this recipe.

Lisa Casey

Pizza Topping Chicken Thighs

In my house we all love pizza and chicken, so I just put the two together and came up with this easy, fast and yummy recipe. It's almost like a chicken Parma.

Serves 4 • Preparation 10 mins • Cook 4 hours • Cooker capacity 5 litres

4 chicken thigh fillets, trimmed
⅔ cup pizza sauce
½ onion, thinly sliced
4 slices ham, chopped
8 button mushrooms, sliced
⅔ cup grated mozzarella cheese

1. Place the chicken between 2 sheets of baking paper and hit with a rolling pin to flatten out slightly. Place into the slow cooker.
2. Spread pizza sauce over the chicken, then top with onion, ham and mushrooms.
3. Cover and cook on LOW for 3½ hours, then add the cheese and cook for another 30 minutes.

NOTE: You could add any 'pizza' toppings you like.

Lisa Casey

Italian Chicken

It's all about easy, healthy and budget-friendly dinners. If you want the quickest prep time ever, this is it!!

Serves 4–6 • Preparation less than 2 minutes! • Cook 6–8 hours • Cooker capacity 5 litres

2 large chicken breast fillets
330 ml (11 fl oz) bottle light Italian dressing
2 cups frozen broccoli
Brown rice, to serve

1. Place the chicken into the slow cooker and pour the Italian dressing over.
2. Cover and cook on LOW for 5 hours.
3. Add the broccoli and cook for 1 hour.
4. To serve, shred the chicken and serve with the broccoli and brown rice.

Steph Watson

Italian Chicken Casserole

I invented this delicious one-pot wonder one day after looking in my fridge and larder to see what I had left before my weekly shop. Staring back at me were the ingredients for a healthy, balanced, family budget meal. Since then it's been a regular favourite in our busy home, especially in cold weather.

Serves 4 • Preparation 15 mins • Cook 5–6 hours • Cooker capacity 4 litres

2 teaspoons oil
8 chicken drumsticks
5 potatoes, cubed
2 carrots, chopped
1 onion, chopped
200 ml (7 fl oz) cream
1 cup dried soup mix (see note)
½ cup chopped parsley
35 g (1 oz) packet cream of chicken soup mix
1 teaspoon dried Italian mixed herbs

1. Heat the oil in a frying pan over medium-high heat. Brown the chicken then transfer to the slow cooker.
2. Add the potatoes, carrots and onion, then stir through the cream, soup mix, parsley, chicken soup mix, Italian herbs and 3 cups water. Season with salt and pepper.
4. Cover and cook on LOW for 5–6 hours. Check sauce and remove the lid for the last 30 minutes of cooking if you prefer a thicker consistency.

NOTE: Soup mix is a mixture of dried split peas, lentils and barley. You'll find it in the soup section at the supermarket. Make sure you don't get the Italian soup mix, as it contains dried beans which are unsuitable for the slow cooker. For younger children remove the meat from the bones just before serving.

Laura Thomson

Sweet Bachicken

There were a few popular chicken and cream cheese dishes on the Facebook group and they were nice, but not quite to our taste. So I thought why not play around with them and find a recipe that suits us. I decided to take a little out of this recipe and add a little to that recipe, and ended up with a dish that we thoroughly enjoy. And the name – sweet bachicken? That was a combination of 'sweet chilli' and 'bacon' and 'chicken'!

Serves 4 • Preparation 15 mins • Cook 2½ hours • Cooker capacity 3.5 litres

700 g (1 lb 2 oz) chicken breast fillets, diced
8 slices salami (we use Hungarian hot)
3 rashers bacon, sliced
¼ cup sweet chilli sauce
½ teaspoon sweet paprika
½ teaspoon chilli flakes
¼ teaspoon red curry paste
250 g (9 oz) cream cheese, cubed
1 teaspoon cornflour (cornstarch), if required
Pasta and steamed vegetables, to serve
Lemon wedges, to serve (optional)

1. Place the chicken, salami and bacon into the slow cooker. Mix the sweet chilli sauce, paprika, chilli flakes and curry paste and pour over the chicken. Stir to combine. Scatter the cream cheese cubes over the mixture.
2. Cover and cook on HIGH for 2 hours. Give mixture a good stir and cook on LOW for 30 minutes. The cream cheese doesn't melt until the last 30 minutes, so a good stir should bring it all together.
3. If the cream cheese has split, try giving it a really good stir to bring it together. If that does not work, then combine the cornflour with 1 tablespoon water until smooth. Add to the chicken mixture and stir well.
4. Serve with pasta and vegetables, and a squeeze of lemon if you like.

NOTE: This dish is quite spicy. Reduce the heat by using a 'mild' sweet chilli sauce, and reducing the amount of chilli flakes and red curry paste.

You can add sun-dried tomatoes, chorizo and/or mushrooms if you like.

It would also be nice served on rice, with naan bread.

Use the AUTO function and cook for 2½ hours if you prefer.

Roslyn Potter

Low carb Creamy Garlic Chicken

When I began following a low carb diet it was a natural progression to experiment with these recipes in my slow cooker also. The creamy garlic sauce in this dish is so tasty, and perfectly complements the chicken. A meal the whole family can enjoy.

Serves 4 • Preparation 15 mins • Cook 2 hours • Cooker capacity 5 litres

1 teaspoon olive oil
700 g (1 lb 9 oz) chicken thigh fillets, cut into small cubes
1 tablespoon minced garlic
300 ml (10 fl oz) cooking cream
1 cup grated tasty cheese, plus extra to serve

1. Heat the oil in a searing slow cooker (or frying pan on the stovetop over medium-high heat) and brown the chicken and garlic.
2. Combine the chicken, garlic and cream in the slow cooker add season with salt and pepper.
3. Cover, putting a tea towel (dish towel) under the lid, and cook on LOW for 2 hours.
4. Add the cheese and stir to melt. Serve sprinkled with extra cheese.

NOTE: This is a great low carb meal when served with the cauliflower mash on page 41.

Paulene Christie

Garlic & Lemon Chicken

This is an experimental recipe I came up with using random things I had in the fridge and cupboard. I was hoping it would turn out to be good, and when it was cooked my family told me it was so good that I had to make it again. Even my fussy daughter eats this.

Serves 4 • Preparation 10 mins • Cook 8 hours • Cooker capacity 6 litres

3 chicken breast fillets, sliced
½ cup lemon juice
¼ cup olive oil
1 tablespoon dried parsley flakes
2–3 teaspoons minced garlic
½ teaspoon salt
¼ teaspoon ground black pepper
Steamed rice, to serve

1. Place all the ingredients into a bowl and mix together until combined. Transfer to the slow cooker.
2. Cover and cook on LOW for 8 hours.
3. Serve with rice.

Trinity Simmons

Slow Cooker Central Cordon Bleu

I'd seen this dish prepared using a stovetop and oven, so I figured why not put my own spin on a slow cooker version. It's great served with a selection of fresh vegetables on the side.

Serves 4–5 • Preparation 15 mins • Cook 1 hour 45 mins • Cooker capacity 7 litres

800 g (1 lb 12 oz) chicken thigh or breast fillets
100 g (3½ oz) thinly sliced ham
80 g (2 ¾ oz) sliced Swiss cheese
1 egg
1½ cups panko breadcrumbs
1 tablespoon Tuscan seasoning
1 teaspoon cracked black pepper

1. Lay one piece of chicken on a sheet of baking paper and top with another sheet. Using a meat mallet or rolling pin, flatten the chicken to a thickness of about 5 mm (¼ inch). Reusing the baking paper, repeat with remaining chicken.
2. Place one slice of ham over each chicken piece, then top with a slice of cheese. Roll the chicken up to enclose the ham and cheese, and fasten with two or more toothpicks.
3. Lightly grease the slow cooker, cover and pre-heat on HIGH.
4. Lightly beat the egg in a bowl. Combine panko, pepper and Tuscan seasoning in a separate bowl. Brush each chicken portion with egg, then roll in the panko mixture to coat.
5. Place into the slow cooker and cook for 1 hour 45 minutes.

NOTE: Adjust times accordingly for smaller cookers.

Simon Christie

Easy Creamy Garlic Chicken

I was searching the internet to find a simple recipe using the few ingredients left in my cupboards. When I couldn't find anything, I made my up own. It came out better than I could have hoped!

Serves 6 • Preparation 10 mins • Cook 5–7 hours • Cooker capacity 6 litres

6 chicken thigh fillets
420 g (15 oz) can condensed cream of chicken soup
6 garlic cloves, minced
2 teaspoons dried oregano
100 g (3½ oz) grated cheddar cheese (optional)
Peas and mashed potato, to serve

1. Place the chicken into the slow cooker. Combine the soup, garlic and oregano. Season with salt and pepper. Pour over the chicken.
2. Cover and cook on LOW for 5–7 hours. Sprinkle with cheese (if using) for the last 30 minutes of cooking.
3. Serve with peas and mashed potato.

Stephanie Brookes

Farmhouse Chicken, Chorizo & Veggie Casserole

I was doing a bit of a fridge, freezer and pantry clean out and came up with this recipe. It's since become a favourite. It's delicious on its own but if you are trying to stretch meals to save money you can serve it with steamed vegetables, mashed or boiled potatoes, pasta, rice or noodles.

Serves 4–6 (with leftovers) • Preparation 10 mins • Cook 8 hours • Cooker capacity 6 litres

1 kg (2 lb 3 oz) chicken breast or thigh fillets
1 chorizo sausage, chopped
2 sweet potatoes, chopped
1 carrot, chopped
420 g (15 oz) can condensed cream of chicken soup
1 onion, chopped
1 tablespoon minced garlic
1 teaspoon wholegrain mustard
½ teaspoon minced ginger
2 cups frozen mixed vegetables
½ cup frozen peas

1. Place the chicken, chorizo, sweet potato and carrot into the slow cooker. Add the soup, onion, garlic, mustard and ginger, and stir gently to combine.
2. Cover and cook on LOW for 6 hours.
3. Add the frozen vegetables, including the peas, and cook for a further 2 hours. You can certainly add them earlier if you need to but they may lose some colour and crunch.

NOTE: You can add any vegetables you have on hand.

Fiona Masters

Danae's Creamy Pesto Chicken Fettuccine

A friend shared a popular creamy pesto chicken recipe with me which I really wanted to try. The recipe wasn't suitable for the slow cooker, or a large family, so I tweaked it a little to suit my catering and budgetary needs!

Serves 6–8 • Preparation 10 mins • Cook 5 hours • Cooker capacity 5 litres

1 kg (2 lb 3 oz) chicken breast fillets, cut into chunks
¼ cup basil pesto (or more, to taste)
1 teaspoon minced garlic (optional)
600 ml (20½ fl oz) cream
300 ml (10½ fl oz) milk
500 g (1 lb 2 oz) tricolour egg fettuccine

1. Mix the chicken, pesto and garlic (if using) and place into the slow cooker.
2. Cover and cook on LOW for 3 hours.
3. Pour in the cream and milk and place the fettuccine on top. Cover and cook for a further 1 hour, or until the pasta can be stirred through.
4. Cover and cook for 1 more hour, until the pasta is cooked.

NOTE: During the last hour of cooking you may sometimes find the pasta needs a dash of extra milk. I have also added a couple of tablespoons of light sour cream which was very delicious.

Danae Weaver

Creamy Tuscan Chicken

This recipe features the most amazing creamy garlic sauce, with the added pizzaz of mushrooms, sun-dried tomatoes and baby spinach. The meal looks and tastes so good, but is cheap and easy to make. I serve it for dinner over jasmine rice, but you could serve it over fettuccine. A family favourite – bon appetit!

Serves 4 • Preparation 10 mins • Cook 3–4 hours • Cooker capacity 6 litres

8 chicken thigh fillets, cut into thick slices
600 ml (20½ fl oz) pure cream
250 g (9 oz) mushrooms, sliced
½ cup sun-dried tomatoes
½ cup cherry tomatoes, halved
3–4 garlic cloves, minced
1 chicken stock cube, crumbled
1 cup baby spinach leaves
Jasmine rice, to serve

1. Combine all the ingredients except the spinach in the slow cooker.
2. Cover and cook on LOW for 3–4 hours.
3. Just before serving, stir in the spinach leaves to wilt. Season with salt and pepper to taste.
4. Serve over rice.

NOTE: If you would like the sauce to be thicker, mix 1 tablespoon of cornflour and 1 tablespoon water in a small bowl until smooth. Stir into the sauce at the end of the cooking time.

Sylvia O'Grady

Chicken & Veg Staples Stew

This recipe is built on the pantry staples you have on hand. You can change the vegetables I've used to whatever you have, so don't worry if they are not exactly the same. Not only is it a great budget meal that's filling and nutritious for the whole family, it's also a great way to use up your leftover vegetables at the end of each week before shopping day. Waste not, want not.

Serves 6 • Preparation 15 mins • Cook 5 hours • Cooker capacity 6 litres

1 kg (2 lb 3 oz) chicken thigh fillets, diced
3 cups chicken stock
3 washed potatoes, cut into 2 cm (¾ inch) cubes
2 carrots, sliced
1 large onion, sliced
1 sweet potato, diced
1 cup diced pumpkin
⅓ cup dried green peas
1 tablespoon minced garlic
40 g (1½ oz) packet chicken noodle soup mix
2 teaspoon each chopped fresh parsley, thyme and garlic chives
Crusty bread rolls, to serve

1. Combine all the ingredients in the slow cooker and season with salt and pepper.
2. Cover and cook on HIGH for 5 hours.
3. Serve with crusty bread rolls to dunk into the sauce.

NOTE: Keep the potato cubes relatively small to ensure they become nice and tender. Use half the amount of dried herbs instead of fresh if you prefer. Cook on LOW for 7 hours if that works better for you.

Paulene Christie

Thai Mango Curry Chicken

This is a simple and subtle recipe, a great way to enjoy authentic Thai flavours from your slow cooker. Easy to prepare and even easier to enjoy.

Serves 4 • Preparation 10 mins • Cook 2½–3 hours • Cooker capacity 3.5 litres

2 teaspoons olive oil
500 g (1 lb 2 oz) chicken breast or thigh fillets, cubed
2 teaspoons red curry paste
400 ml (13½ fl oz) can coconut cream
1 red capsicum (pepper), sliced
2 ripe mangoes, sliced (or 1 can, drained)
Rice, to serve

1. Heat the olive oil in a large non-stick frying pan and cook the chicken until browned. Add the curry paste and fry for 1–2 minutes, until fragrant.
2. Transfer to the slow cooker. Add the coconut cream and capsicum and stir well.
3. Cover and cook on HIGH for 2 hours.
4. Add the mangoes and cook on LOW for 30–60 minutes. Serve on a bed of rice.

Jenny Krahe

Creamy Chicken with Asparagus, Bacon & Sun-dried Tomato

I was struggling with ways to use up some asparagus and spinach soup that I didn't think I'd like just on its own. A very good friend of mine who is a chef talked me through some great flavour combinations to try with it and this creamy, flavour packed dish was the result. Delicious!

Serves 6 • Preparation 10 mins • Cook 5 hours • Cooker capacity 5 litres

1 kg (2 lb 3 oz) chicken thigh fillets
400 g (14 oz) pouch/can asparagus & spinach soup
250 g (9 oz) block light cream cheese
200 g (7 oz) diced bacon
100 g (3½ oz) sun-dried tomatoes (in vinegar, patted dry)
2 teaspoons minced garlic
Pasta or mashed potato and steamed vegetables, to serve

1. Place all the ingredients into the slow cooker and season with salt and pepper.
2. Cover and cook on HIGH for 2 hours, then reduce to LOW and cook for 3 hours.
3. Serve with pasta or mashed potato and steamed vegetables.

NOTE: I found the sauce didn't need any thickening as it was lovely and thick and creamy.

Paulene Christie

Creamy Hasselback Chicken

I've tried quite a few different hasselback chicken recipes and this is by far my favourite. It's very popular with the slow cooker group. If you don't like it spicy just leave out the Cajun seasoning.

Serves 4 • Preparation 15 minutes • Cook 3–4 hours • Cooker capacity 5 litres

4 chicken breast fillets
4 cheese slices (any type you like), sliced
4 rashers shortcut bacon, sliced
2 cups cooking cream
¼ cup sweet chilli sauce
1 teaspoon minced garlic
1 teaspoon Cajun seasoning
Dried or fresh chives, to taste

1. Make deep cuts crossways into the chicken fillets, making sure you don't cut all the way through. Place cheese and bacon into the cuts.
2. Lay the chicken into the slow cooker. Mix all the other ingredients in a bowl, season with pepper, then pour around the chicken.
3. Cover and cook on LOW for 3–4 hours.

NOTE: At the end of cooking if the creamy sauce is watery, stir 1 tablespoon cornflour (cornstarch) with 1 tablespoon water until smooth. Stir into the sauce to thicken.

Lisa Casey

Chantelle's Chicken Curry

This recipe is a family favourite in our home – even my fussy three year old loves it. It's nice and easy to prepare and the flavours are amazing!

Serves 4 • Preparation 15 mins • Cook 4–6 hours • Cooker capacity 5.5 litres

500 g (1 lb 2 oz) chicken thigh fillets, diced
1 large potato, diced
2 carrots, diced
2 tablespoons oil
1 large brown onion, chopped
2 tablespoons minced garlic
2 tablespoons curry powder
1 teaspoon garam masala
1 teaspoon ground cumin
1 teaspoon ground coriander
400 g (14 oz) can diced tomatoes
400 ml (13½ fl oz) can coconut cream
Rice and naan bread, to serve

1. Place the chicken, potato and carrots into the slow cooker.
2. Heat the oil in a small frying over medium heat. Cook the onion and garlic until translucent.
3. Add the curry powder and other spices to the onion and stir. Continue cooking for one minute. Stir in the tomatoes.
4. Pour the tomato mixture over the chicken and vegetables and mix well.
5. Cover and cook on LOW for 4–6 hours. Stir in the coconut cream for the last 15 minutes of cooking.
6. Serve with rice and naan bread.

NOTE: You can add any other vegetables you like to bulk up the meal. It also freezes well, so it makes excellent leftovers.

Chantelle Ogier

Coconut Cashew Chicken

This dish is beautiful and my children love it. It combines the great flavours of cashews and coconut.

Serves 6–8 • Preparation 15 mins • Cook 4–5 hours • Cooker capacity 5.5 litres

1 kg (2 lb 3 oz) chicken thigh fillets, cut into small pieces
1 large onion, diced
1 cup cashews
400 ml (13 ⅓ fl oz) can coconut cream
2 tablespoons tomato paste
2 tablespoons minced garlic
2 teaspoons soy sauce
1 teaspoon ground turmeric
½ teaspoon garlic powder
½ teaspoon Worcestershire sauce
Rice and stir-fried vegetables, to serve

1. Place the chicken and onion into the slow cooker and season well with salt and pepper.
2. Combine ¾ cup of the cashews and the remaining ingredients in a blender and blend until smooth. Pour over the chicken.
3. Cover and cook on LOW for 4–5 hours.
4. Stir in the remaining cashews and serve with rice and stir-fried vegetables.

NOTE: Cook on HIGH for 2–3 hours if you prefer.

Lynda Eagleson

Festive Chicken & Stuffing

This meal has everything you need for a festive holiday dinner. It's tasty, easy to make and budget-wise. The chicken is tender, the gravy thick and the stuffing steamed and soft. The hero of this dish – the cranberries ! As it cooks the house is filled with a divine smell – definitely a family pleaser.

Serves 4 • Preparation 10 mins • Cook 4–5 hours • Cooker capacity 6 litres

3 tablespoons chicken gravy powder (I use Supreme Chicken)
4 chicken breast fillets
150 g (5½ oz) seasoned stuffing mix
60 g (2 oz) dried cranberries
50 g (1 ¾ oz) butter, melted
Roast vegetables or steamed green beans, to serve

1. Mix the gravy powder with 1 cup water and pour into the slow cooker. Place the chicken breasts in a row over the gravy.
2. Sprinkle the stuffing mix over the chicken, to generously cover. Sprinkle the cranberries on top, and drizzle with butter.
3. Cover and cook on LOW for 4–5 hours.
4. Serve with roast vegetables or steamed green beans.

Sylvia O'Grady

Chicken Paprikash

My heritage is Hungarian and I wanted to be able to cook an old family favourite in my slow cooker. I have managed to come up with a winning recipe that came out better than the original (sorry Mum). This one is now top of my slow cooker recipe list. Hungarian comfort food at its finest!

Serves 4–6 • Preparation 10 mins • Cook 6 hours • Cooker capacity 5 litres

1.5 kg (3 lb 5 oz) chicken pieces, bone in
4 tablespoons Hungarian paprika (sweet or hot depending on taste)
2 teaspoons onion powder
1 teaspoon caraway seeds
1 teaspoon salt
½ teaspoon dried marjoram
½ teaspoon garlic powder
400 g (14 oz) can diced tomatoes
¼ cup plain (all-purpose) flour
600 g (1 lb 5 oz) sour cream
Rice or egg noodles, to serve

1. Place the chicken pieces into the slow cooker and add the paprika, onion powder, caraway seeds, salt, marjoram and garlic powder. Add the tomatoes and two cans of water. Mix to incorporate the seasonings.
2. Cover and cook on LOW for 5½ hours.
3. Whisk the flour with ½ cup water and add to slow cooker. Add the sour cream and stir to combine. Cover and cook a further 30 minutes.
4. Serve over rice or egg noodles.

NOTE: Chicken thigh fillets would work well too. You can use stock instead of water if you prefer.

Renee Garth

Slow Cooked Camembert Chicken Mignon

This is a delightful variation on a traditional chicken mignon dinner, perfect with a side of fresh vegetables or a light salad. Adults and children alike will find this a favourite.

Serves 4 • Preparation 10 mins • Cook 4 hours • Cooker capacity 5 litres

4 chicken breast fillets
100 g (3½ oz) camembert
4 rashers bacon

1. Trim any fat from the chicken. Using a small sharp knife, cut a deep pocket into the side of each chicken breast.
2. Cut the camembert into four equal parts and place one piece into each pocket. Wrap a bacon rasher around each chicken breast, and fix in place using two toothpicks.
3. Place into the slow cooker, ensuring the breast pockets are facing up so you don't lose the cheesy goodness.
4. Cover and cook on HIGH for 4 hours.

Simon Christie

Mediterranean Creamy Chicken

This is a family favourite. With chicken breasts being reasonably priced and often on sale it fits the budget. We always have enough for leftovers. Winning!

Serves 6 • Preparation 10 mins • Cook 3–4 hours • Cooker capacity 6 litres

600 ml (20½ fl oz) cooking cream
200 g (7 oz) mushrooms, sliced
125 g (4½ oz) sun-dried tomatoes, chopped
100 g (3½ oz) cherry tomatoes, chopped
100 g (3½ oz) mixed olives (optional)
3–4 garlic cloves, minced
1 kg (2 lb 3 oz) chicken breast fillets, cut into large chunks
Rice, to serve

1. Mix the cream, mushrooms, sun-dried tomatoes, cherry tomatoes, olives and garlic together to make a sauce. Place half of this mixture into the slow cooker.
2. Add the chicken and cover with the remaining sauce.
3. Cover and cook on LOW for 3–4 hours.
4. Serve with rice

Mel Crean

Chicken, Bacon & Mushroom Tagliatelle

This mix of ingredients always seems to end up making a meal taste delicious. It's tried and tested, and always cooked just right.

Serves 4 • Preparation 10 mins • Cook 4–5 hours • Cooker capacity 3.5 litres

5 small chicken breast fillets, cubed
2 x 500 g (1 lb 2 oz) jars carbonara sauce
500 g (1 lb 2 oz) chopped bacon
10 mushrooms, sliced
250 g (9 oz) fresh tagliatelle

1. Combine the chicken, carbonara sauce, bacon and mushrooms in the slow cooker.
2. Cover and cook on LOW for 4–5 hours, adding the tagliatelle 30 minutes before serving.

Lisa Pittaway

Thai Green Chicken Curry

I am a relatively new convert to Thai food but a green chicken curry is by far my favourite dish. This version is mild enough for the whole family to enjoy, but incorporates the lovely Thai flavours you want from such a dish. A great option for entertaining or when you want to enjoy the taste of take-away made at home.

Serves 6 • Preparation 20 mins • Cook 6 hours • Cooker capacity 5 litres

1 kg (2 lb 3 oz) chicken thigh fillets
100 g (3½ oz) green beans, trimmed and halved
½ eggplant, cubed
½ green capsicum (pepper) cut into strips
2 kaffir lime leaves, cut into fine strips
1 tablespoon fish sauce
1 tablespoon lime juice
800 ml (27 fl oz) coconut milk
⅓ cup Thai green curry paste
1 tbsp cornflour (cornstarch)
1 bunch broccolini, trimmed, cut into florets
1 zucchini, halved and sliced
1 bunch buk choy, trimmed
60 g (2 oz) baby spinach leaves
Lime wedges, to serve

1. Place the chicken, beans, eggplant, capsicum, lime leaves, fish sauce and lime juice into the slow cooker. Whisk the coconut milk, curry paste and cornflour together and add to the slow cooker.
2. Cover and cook on LOW for 4½ hours.
3. Add the broccolini and zucchini and cook for 30 minutes.
4. Add the buk choy and spinach and cook for a further 1 hour.
5. Serve with fresh lime wedges for a beautiful Thai taste!

Paulene Christie

PORK & BACON

Bacon & Zucchini Pie

I was looking for a lovely summery dish to impress the family and decided to make a few additions to a zucchini pie I had made over the years. Serve this with your favourite sides.

Serves 6 • Preparation 20 mins • Cook 4 hours • Cooker capacity 6.5 litres

1 onion, grated
1 carrot, grated
2 zucchini
6 rashers bacon, diced
½ chorizo sausage, diced
1 cup grated tasty cheese
1½ cups milk
4 eggs
½ cup plain (all-purpose) flour

1. Grate the zucchini and squeeze out the excess liquid.
2. Line the slow cooker with baking paper and layer in the onion, carrot, zucchini, bacon, chorizo and cheese.
3. Combine the milk, eggs and flour in a jug, and season with salt and pepper. Pour over the ingredients in the slow cooker (no need to stir).
4. Cover, putting a tea towel (dish towel) under the lid, and cook on LOW for 4 hours.

NOTE: Add raw sausage chunks to the slow cooker at the beginning for an extra meaty version.

Denise Roberts

Trinity's Carbonara

I'm not a fan of the traditional carbonara sauces, so my mum and I decided to make our own. We think it tastes so much better than anything store-bought or from a restaurant. My entire family loves this recipe. There's nothing better than home-made carbonara – yummy.

Serves 4–8 • Preparation 10 mins • Cook 2½ hours • Cooker capacity 6 litres

400 g (14 oz) bacon pieces
2 onions, chopped
4 garlic cloves, minced
2 x 375 ml (12½ fl oz) cans evaporated milk
1 cup shredded tasty cheese
2–3 tablespoons shredded parmesan cheese
Pasta, to serve

1. Cook the bacon, onion and garlic in a frying pan to a nice golden brown colour.
2. Pour the evaporated milk into the slow cooker then stir in the bacon mixture and cheeses.
3. Cover and cook on LOW for 2½ hours, stirring every 15–30 minutes.
4. Serve over pasta.

Trinity Simmons

BBQ Honey Pork

This is a great family favourite – simple and easy to make with few ingredients.

Serves 6 • Preparation 15 mins • Cook 6 – 6½ hours • Cooker capacity 5 litres

2 teaspoons oil
6 large pork chops (forequarter recommended)
1 cup BBQ sauce
¾ cup honey
Splash of Worcestershire sauce
1 garlic clove, thinly sliced

1. Heat the oil in a large frying pan and brown the pork in batches. Transfer to the slow cooker. Add the BBQ sauce, honey, Worcestershire sauce and garlic.
2. Cover and cook on LOW for 6–6½ hours, until tender.

Vicky Grindal

Pork Chops with Apple & Onion Gravy

This is a great family friendly recipe for busy people on the go. I love pork chops but my family not so much. I'm always trying to come up with a recipe to suit all our fussy eaters and this was a winner all round!

Serves 4 • Preparation 10 mins • Cook 4–6 hours • Cooker capacity 6 litres

2 green apples, cored and sliced, skin on
1 large brown onion, sliced
4 pork chops
2 cups thick gravy
1 tablespoon Worcestershire sauce
2 teaspoons minced garlic
1 teaspoon Dijon mustard
Mashed potatoes and steamed veggies, to serve

1. Place the apples and onion into the slow cooker, and put the pork chops on top.
2. Combine the remaining ingredients and pour over the pork.
3. Cover and cook on LOW for 4–6 hours (depending on your slow cooker).
4. Remove the pork chops. Using a potato masher, roughly mash the apple and onion into the gravy. Serve with mashed potato and steamed veggies.

Kylie McPherson

Spicy Hoisin Pork Chops

My family love pork chops and I wanted to try something different, so I came up with this. You can have it as spicy as you like – hubby and I love it spicy and served on mashed potatoes.

Serves 4 • Preparation 5 mins • Cook 5 hours • Cooker capacity 5 litres

4 pork chops, rind removed
1 cup hoisin sauce
½ cup BBQ sauce
1 teaspoon minced garlic
½ teaspoon ground chilli (or to taste)
2 teaspoons cornflour (cornstarch)

1. Place the pork chops into the slow cooker. Mix the sauces, garlic and chilli together, season with pepper and pour over the pork chops.
2. Cover and cook on LOW for 5 hours.
3. Remove pork chops and set aside. Mix cornflour with 2 teaspoons water until smooth. Stir into sauce to thicken.

Lisa Casey

Creamy Mustard Pork Chops

I created this French-inspired dish in memory of those lost in the terrorist attacks that struck Paris in 2015. Follow it up with the French Toast Dessert on page 256.

Serves 4 • Preparation 15 mins • Cook 2½ hours • Cooker capacity 5 litres

4 pork loin chops
1 teaspoon salt
1 teaspoon ground black pepper
½ cup dry white wine
1½ tablespoons Dijon mustard
1 teaspoon chopped fresh tarragon
½ cup finely sliced eschalots
2 tablespoons double cream
4 cups rocket (arugula)
Lemon wedges, to serve

1. Heat a searing slow cooker (or frying pan on the stovetop over medium-high heat). Season the chops with salt and pepper, and cook until brown.
2. Mix the wine, mustard and tarragon in a jug and pour over the chops in the slow cooker.
3. Cover, putting a tea towel (dish towel) under the lid, and cook on LOW for 1 hour 15 minutes.
4. Turn chops and increase to HIGH. Cook, covered with lid and tea towel, for 1 hour.
5. Stir in eschalots and cream, and cook uncovered for 10–15 minutes, until sauce has thickened.
6. Serve chops drizzled with sauce, with rocket leaves and lemon wedges.

Simon Christie

Creamy Pork Chops

This is my all-time favourite slow cooker recipe, and my whole family loves it. The pork always comes out tender. You could even add bacon.

Serves 2–4 • Preparation 10 mins • Cook 4–5 hours • Cooker capacity 5 litres

2–4 pork chops, rind removed
5–6 mushrooms, sliced
1 small onion, sliced
½ capsicum (pepper), diced
300 ml (10 fl oz) cooking cream
40 g (1½ oz) packet French onion soup mix
1 teaspoon Cajun seasoning
1 teaspoon garlic salt

1. Place pork chops into the slow cooker. Arrange mushrooms, onion and capsicum on top.
2. Mix the remaining ingredients in a bowl and season with cracked pepper. Pour over the chops and vegetables.
3. Cover and cook on LOW for 4–5 hours.

Lisa Casey

Pineapple & Brown Sugar Christmas Ham

This is a great dish to pop in the slow cooker on Christmas morning because it will be ready for Christmas lunch. Let your Christmas lunch cook while you open presents! This ham is sweet tasting and will go perfectly with salad and roast vegetables. Drizzle sauce over the ham before serving for a sweet glaze.

Serves 6 • Preparation 10 mins • Cook 6–8 hours • Cooker capacity 7 litres

2 cups brown sugar
1 ham (preferably boneless in case you need to trim to fit into slow cooker)
450 g (15½ oz) can pineapple, undrained
Fresh pineapple, to serve (optional)

1. Spread a thin, even layer of brown sugar over the base of the slow cooker. Place the ham on top of the brown sugar.
2. Place the pineapple on top of the ham and drizzle the juice from the can all over the ham. Top with the remaining sugar.
3. Cover and cook on LOW for 6–8 hours.
4. Drizzle the sauce over the top of ham before serving, and char-grill fresh pineapple (if using) for the perfect presentation.

Mel Ireland

Sticky Chinese Pork Belly

This is a succulent sticky Chinese pork belly that will melt in your mouth and win your heart, with a sauce that will have you coming back for more.

Serves 4 • Preparation 10 mins + marinating • Cook 4 hours • Cooker capacity 5.5 litres

⅓ cup soy sauce
¼ cup honey
2 tablespoons brown sugar
2 tablespoons rice wine
5 cm (2 inch) piece fresh ginger, finely grated
3 garlic cloves, minced
1 red chilli, finely chopped
1 kg (2 lb 3 oz) pork belly, cut into 4 cm (1 ¾ inch) cubes
1 cup chicken or vegetable stock

1. Combine the soy sauce, honey, sugar, rice wine, ginger, garlic and chilli in a shallow non-metallic dish and season with salt and pepper. Add pork cubes and mix well. Cover and place into the fridge for a few hours to marinate.
2. Transfer pork, marinade and stock to the slow cooker.
3. Cover and cook on LOW for 3 hours. Place a tea towel (dish towel) under the lid and cook for a further 1 hour.

TIP: For a thicker sauce, pour liquid into a saucepan. Mix 1 tablespoon cornflour (cornstarch) with 1 tablespoon water until smooth. Add to the pan and stir over medium-high heat until thickened.

Denise Roberts

Sweet Chilli Pork Chops

This is one of my favourite pork chop recipes. The sauce is mild enough for the whole family but you could increase the heat factor with a hotter sweet chilli sauce if you prefer. We like to serve ours with mashed potato and vegetables as the sauce is divine spooned over the mash! You can change the number of pork chops to suit your family as there is plenty of sauce in the recipe. Use whatever cut of pork chop you prefer or whatever kind is on special at your butcher to keep it within your budget.

Serves 6 • Preparation 10 mins • Cook 6 hours • Cooker capacity 6 litres

6 pork chops
1 large onion, cut into thin strips
½ cup mild sweet chilli sauce
¼ cup hoisin sauce
1 tablespoon minced garlic
1 teaspoon sesame oil

1. Place pork chops into the slow cooker and scatter the onion strips on top. Combine the remaining ingredients and pour over.
2. Cover and cook on LOW for 6 hours.

NOTE: If your sauce is runny at the end of cooking time, transfer the pork chops to serving plates and keep warm. Increase slow cooker to HIGH. Mix 1 tablespoon cornflour (cornstarch) with 1 tablespoon water until smooth. Add to slow cooker and cook, stirring, for about 5 minutes or until thickened.

Paulene Christie

LAMB & GAME

Moroccan Lamb Chops

This is an easy and delicious way to cook cheap lamb chops. I came up with the idea because I was sick of eating boring tough lamb chops. I love the spicy flavour but it's not hot, just creamy and delicious. We probably have it every couple of weeks because we like it so much, served with salad or steamed veg.

Serves 4 • Preparation 10 mins • Cook 4–5 hours • Cooker capacity 5 litres

1 tablespoon olive oil
1 onion, chopped
4 lamb chops
2 tablespoons Moroccan seasoning
400 g (14 oz) can diced tomatoes
400 ml (13½ fl oz) can coconut cream
Couscous, vegetables or salad, and coriander (cilantro), to serve

1. Heat the olive oil in a large frying pan over medium heat. Cook the onion for about 3 minutes, until soft. Add the lamb chops and sprinkle the Moroccan seasoning over. Cook for a couple of minutes each side, until browned.
2. Transfer chops and onion to the slow cooker. Add the tomatoes and coconut cream to the frying pan and stir to combine all the flavours. Pour over the chops.
3. Cover and cook on LOW for 4–5 hours.
4. Serve with couscous and vegetables or salad, sprinkled with coriander.

Kym Byrne

Braised Lamb Chops

I love this recipe because it's such a rich, delicious dish, and it's done on a shoestring budget using cheap lamb chops with minimal ingredients. I came up with this because I wanted a quicker and easier braised chop recipe than the traditional stovetop method. It's a favourite in our home.

Serves 4–6 • Preparation 5 mins • Cook 6 hours • Capacity 3 litres

4–6 cheap lamb chops, such as forequarter, shoulder or neck
2 onions, sliced
1 teaspoon dried rosemary
½ teaspoon dried thyme
400 g (14 oz) can whole tomatoes
2 tablespoons Worcestershire sauce
1 teaspoon beef stock powder
Mashed potato and vegetables or salad, to serve
1 tablespoon cornflour (corn starch)

1. Place the chops into the slow cooker and arrange the onions over the top. Sprinkle with the dried herbs.
2. Combine the tomatoes, Worcestershire sauce, stock powder and ½ cup water. Pour into the slow cooker.
3. Cover and cook on LOW for 6 hours.
4. When 30 minutes from cooked, mix the cornflour with a little water to make a paste and add to the slow cooker. Stir to thicken.
5. Serve with mashed potato, and vegetables or salad.

NOTE: You can use fresh herbs; just double the quantity of the dried.

Kirsten Crack

Lamb Stew

This is a frugal lamb neck chop stew, to use up cheaper cuts of meat we had left over. It was made up as a bit of a mish-mash of things I had lying around when money was tight, but has became a firm favourite. Best served on a cold winter's day or any time you want to put dinner on in the morning and forget about it until dinner time!

Serves 4–6 • Preparation 20 mins • Cook 6–8 hours • Cooker capacity 5.5 litres

3 tablespoons Lancashire relish (see note)
2 tablespoons tomato paste (concentrated puree)
3 teaspoons minced garlic
6–8 lamb neck chops
5 cups thick gravy
2 potatoes, diced
2 carrots, cut into thick slices
1 sweet potato, diced
10 button mushrooms, quartered
3 bay leaves
1 teaspoon dried rosemary leaves

1. Combine the relish, tomato paste and garlic in a large frying pan and stir over medium high-heat for 2 minutes.
2. Add the chops to the pan (in batches), stir in 2 cups of gravy and cook for about 30 seconds each side, until browned. Set the chops aside.
3. Stir the remaining gravy into the mixture in the pan, and remove from the heat.
4. Place the vegetables into the slow cooker and lay the chops on top. Pour the gravy mixture over, and add the herbs.
5. Cover and cook on HIGH for 6–8 hours.

NOTE: Lancashire relish is like Worcestershire sauce, only milder and more fruity. You'll find it near the sauces at the supermarket. If you like, add a chopped capsicum for the last hour of cooking. It is best to mix it through the vegetables underneath the chops.

Helen Prior

Red Wine Rabbit Stew

My partner goes out hunting and my mum requested he get her some rabbits. This is a hearty dish which is great for the whole family, full of divine flavour.

Serves 4 • Preparation 20 mins • Cook 8 hours • Cooker capacity 6 litres

4 potatoes, cut into cubes
3 celery stalks, sliced
3 carrots, diced
1 onion, diced
1 cup mixed frozen corn and peas
1 sweet potato, diced
1 cup chopped beans
12 cups vegetable stock
1 cup red wine
3 bay leaves
1 teaspoon dried basil
1 rabbit, jointed
2 tablespoons cornflour (cornstarch)

1. Combine the vegetables in the slow cooker. Add the stock, wine and 4 cups water.
2. Stir in the bay leaves and basil. Place the rabbit on top and season with salt and pepper.
3. Cover and cook on HIGH for 6 hours, then reduce to LOW and cook for 2 hours.
4. Remove the rabbit from the slow cooker. Mix the cornflour with 2 tablespoons water until smooth, then stir into the liquid to thicken.
5. Serve rabbit and vegetables with the sauce.

Alana Harris

Lamb Chop Casserole

This is a cheap and very easy recipe – you could even use chicken legs instead of lamb if you like.

Serves 2–4 • Preparation 5 mins • Cook: 5 hours • Cooker capacity 5 litres

6 lamb chops
2 x 400 g (14 oz) cans diced tomatoes
40 g (1½ oz) packet French onion soup mix
¼ cup Worcestershire sauce
2 cups chopped frozen vegetables

1. Place the chops into the slow cooker. Combine the tomatoes, soup mix and Worcestershire sauce, and pour over the chops. Season with cracked black pepper.
2. Cover and cook on LOW for 4 hours.
3. Add the vegetables and cook for 1 hour.

Lisa Casey

Roast Lamb with Rosemary Butter & Red Wine Sauce

This is a beautiful, flavour-packed roast lamb – straight from your slow cooker. The rosemary and red wine flavours complement it beautifully, and go together to form a lush gravy. The red wine is subtle enough for the whole family to enjoy. We have empty plates all round when this is served at our house.

Serves 6 • Preparation 10 mins • Cook 5 hours • Cooker capacity 5 litres

1.5 kg (3 lb 5 oz) half leg lamb roast
1½ tablespoons soft butter
1 teaspoon dried rosemary (or 2 teaspoons fresh)
1 heaped teaspoon minced garlic
¼ tsp each of salt and cracked black pepper
½ cup red wine, such as Shiraz
1 tablespoon vegetable stock powder
1 tablespoon tomato paste (concentrated puree)
1 tablespoon cornflour (cornstarch)

1. Place the lamb into the slow cooker. Combine the butter, rosemary, garlic, salt and pepper and mix well. Use a spoon to spread the butter mixture over the top and sides of the lamb.
2. Place the wine, stock powder, tomato paste and ¾ cup hot water into a jug and stir well to combine. Pour into the slow cooker around the lamb (but not over the butter).
3. Cover and cook on HIGH for 5 hours. Baste the meat with the cooking juices occasionally if you are around to do so.
4. Just before serving, remove the lamb from the slow cooker. Use a large spoon to scoop out and discard the excess fat from the surface of the liquid in the slow cooker.
5. Mix the cornflour with 1 tablespoon water until smooth, then stir through the liquid in the slow cooker. If you have a searing slow cooker, place onto the stovetop and simmer to reduce and thicken the sauce. Alternatively, transfer mixture to a saucepan.

NOTE: If like me you don't regularly drink wine you can purchase an inexpensive bottle of Shiraz for around $5. It will keep for a few months in the fridge – not great for drinking but fine for cooking.

Paulene Christie

Lamb & Bacon

Lamb and bacon – two of my favourite foods in one pot. I made this casserole especially for my own selfish reasons: so I could put these two together. I wasn't disappointed! Serve with vegetables and mash for a hearty main meal.

Serves 4 • Preparation 10 mins • Cook 4 hours • Cooker capacity 5 litres

4 lamb forequarter chops (about 800 g/1 lb 12 oz)
6 rashers shortcut bacon (about 200 g/7 oz), roughly chopped
2 carrots, sliced
400 g (14 oz) can diced tomatoes
½ cup sliced spring onions (scallions)
1½ tablespoons reduced-salt soy sauce
1½ tablespoons Worcestershire sauce
1 tablespoon fresh rosemary

1. Heat the oil in a searing slow cooker (or in a frying pan on the stove) and sear the lamb until brown. Drain the excess fat.
2. Combine the lamb and remaining ingredients in the slow cooker.
3. Cover and cook on LOW for 4 hours.

NOTE: Add 1 hour to the cooking time if you decide not to brown the lamb first. Add extra lamb chops for more people – the sauce will be enough to cover them.

Simon Christie

Slow Cooked Lamb Leg

Who doesn't love a leg of lamb? This lamb is beautifully slow-cooked, and is so tender it melts in your mouth. I love the combined flavours of mint, rosemary, garlic and lemon.

Serves 8–10 • Preparation 10 mins • Cook 8 hours • Cooker capacity 5.5 litres

1 lamb leg
5 sprigs fresh rosemary
5 sprigs fresh mint
2 tablespoons olive oil
1 tablespoon lemon juice
1 tablespoon finely grated lemon rind
3 teaspoons minced garlic
1 cup beef stock
¼ cup gravy powder

1. Cut 10 deep slits into the lamb and push the rosemary and mint sprigs into them.
2. Combine the olive oil, lemon juice, lemon rind and garlic. Rub all over the lamb, and season with salt and pepper. Place lamb into the slow cooker and add the stock.
3. Cover and cook on LOW for 8 hours.
4. Remove the lamb from the slow cooker. In a small bowl, mix the gravy powder with a little of the liquid from the slow cooker to make a smooth paste. Stir into the liquid in the slow cooker to thicken.
5. Carve the lamb and serve with the gravy.

NOTE: Leftover lamb is delicious made into sandwiches.

Lynda Eagleson

Lamb Rogan Josh

I love a good curry but not a spicy one. This rogan josh is a mild curry and my children love it as well. The flavours combine beautifully and the smell is amazing as it cooks. This is lovely served with rice, and naan bread or pappadums or both.

Serves 6 • Preparation 20 mins • Cook 6 hours • Cooker capacity 5.5 litres

1 tablespoon olive oil
2 onions, sliced
½ cup rogan josh curry paste
1 kg (2 lb 3 oz) lamb, diced
400 g (14 oz) can diced tomatoes
300 ml (10 fl oz) coconut cream
3 potatoes, diced
2 carrots, sliced
3 tablespoons brown sugar
1 cup beef stock
2 tablespoons ground coriander
2 tablespoons minced garlic
1 tablespoon minced ginger
Chopped peanuts, steamed rice, naan bread and coriander (cilantro) leaves, to serve

1. Heat the oil in a large deep frying pan over medium heat and cook the onions until soft. Add the curry paste and stir for 30 seconds, until fragrant.
2. Add the lamb and cook, stirring to coat in the spice mixture, until just brown. Transfer to the slow cooker, add the remaining ingredients and stir to combine.
3. Cover and cook on LOW for 6 hours.
4. Sprinkle with peanuts and serve with rice, naan bread and coriander leaves.

NOTE: If you want to thicken the sauce at the end of cooking, mix 2 tablespoons of cornflour (cornstarch) with 1 tablespoon water until smooth, then stir into the curry.

Lynda Eagleson

Goat Delight

This is a yummy game-meat recipe, full of flavour. I made it up for my mum and partner.

Serves 4 • Preparation 20 mins • Cook 7 hours • Cooker capacity 6 litres

4 potatoes, cut into large pieces
4 large pieces pumpkin (squash)
2 sweet potatoes, cut into large pieces
1 goat leg
4 cups beef stock
2 tablespoons mint sauce
2 teaspoons dried Italian herbs
Few sprigs fresh mint
Few sprigs fresh rosemary
2 tablespoons cornflour (cornstarch)

1. Roll some balls of foil and place over the base of the slow cooker. Arrange the vegetables over the foil, then place the goat leg on top.
2. Combine the stock and mint sauce, and add to the slow cooker. Sprinkle dried herbs over the goat and add the fresh mint and rosemary.
3. Cover and cook on HIGH for 6 hours. Reduce to LOW and cook for 1 hour.
4. Remove goat and vegetables from the slow cooker, and discard the foil. Mix the cornflour with 2 tablespoons water until smooth, then stir into the liquid to thicken.
5. Serve goat and vegetables with the sauce.

NOTE: Add ½ cup red wine with the stock, if you like.

Alana Harris

Rustic Lamb Casserole

There's something about slow cooked lamb. It's just so tender and juicy. Packing it with vegetables makes a filling, nutritious, one-pot meal to fill the whole family on a small budget. We serve this in bowls with crusty bread rolls for mopping up the sauce. You can cook it for longer on LOW if you need an all-day recipe.

Serves 8 • Preparation 15 mins • Cook 6 hours • Cooker capacity 6 litres

1 kg (2 lb 3 oz) diced lamb
4–6 small washed potatoes, skin left on, roughly chopped
4 thin carrots, roughly chopped
1½ cups diced pumpkin
1 cup frozen peas
2 cups vegetable stock
2 tablespoons tomato paste (concentrated puree)
2 tablespoons Worcestershire sauce
2 tablespoons mint sauce
1 tablespoon fresh thyme leaves
Crusty bread, to serve

1. Combine all the ingredients in the slow cooker and season with freshly ground black pepper.
2. Cover and cook on HIGH for 6 hours. Stir once or twice during cooking, taking care not to break up the vegetables.
3. Serve with crusty bread.

NOTE: You could also easily cook this on LOW for 8–10 hours.

Paulene Christie

SEAFOOD

Crustless Crab Quiche

Growing up in Hervey Bay I was lucky to be raised eating a lot of local fresh mud crab that my Dad caught on Fraser Island. These days I'm not so lucky as to enjoy fresh crab very often, so using canned crab meat or seafood extender is a budget-friendly alternative. This quiche looks and sounds fancy – but with minimal effort required. The proof is in the tasting – so good! This could also be made into mini quiches in silicone muffin cases, or made in one large block and served cut into small squares.

Serves 6 • Preparation 10 mins • Cook 1 hour • Cooker capacity 7 litres

4 eggs
½ cup thickened (whipping) cream
1 cup seafood extender (or fresh or canned crab meat)
⅔ cup grated Swiss cheese
12 chives, chopped
¼ teaspoon garlic powder
Spray oil

1. Whisk the eggs and cream together in a mixing bowl. Cut the crab meat or seafood extender into thin ribbons and stir through.
2. Add the cheese, chives and garlic powder. Season with salt and pepper and stir to combine.
3. Spray a silicone flan dish (or whatever you wish to cook your quiche in) well with oil. Pour the mixture into the prepared dish and carefully place into the slow cooker.
4. Cover, putting a tea towel (dish towel) under the lid, and cook on HIGH for 1 hour or until set.

NOTE: You could also cook this directly in your slow cooker on a lining of baking paper.

Paulene Christie

Seafood Sticks

I made this recipe one day when I had a packet of seafood sticks that I wasn't sure what to do with. My kids love seafood sticks from the corner store but I wasn't keen on them eating too many of the deep-fried version – not to mention the cost! This was a much better alternative. It's so simple that they can even cook it themselves with my supervision, which they love doing.

Makes 8 • Preparation 15 mins • Cook 1 hour 15 mins • Cooker capacity 7 litres

2 sheets frozen puff pastry
8 seafood sticks
1 egg, lightly beaten
Spray oil

1. Lay the pastry out on the bench and cut into quarters using a sharp knife. Place one seafood stick diagonally across each square.
2. Roll each seafood stick up in the pastry and pinch the ends to enclose and seal. Pierce along the top of each parcel with a fork 2–3 times. Brush with egg.
3. Spray the slow cooker bowl lightly with oil, or line with baking paper. Place the parcels into the slow cooker.
4. Cover, putting a tea towel (dish towel) under the lid, and cook on HIGH for 30 minutes. Turn the sticks over and brush again with egg. Cook for a further 30 minutes, turn and brush again, then cook for a final 15 minutes. Serve hot.

Paulene Christie

Sweet Chilli Basted Fish

This is a delicious summer meal. The sauce works on any type of fish and the texture is amazing – moist and never dried out.

Serves 4 • Preparation 20 mins • Cook 2 hours • Cooker capacity 6 litres

Spray olive oil
4 fish steaks or fillets, skin on
Lemon slices
2–3 spring onions (scallions), chopped
¼ cup tomato sauce (ketchup)
2 tablespoons sweet chilli sauce
1 tablespoon brown sugar
2 teaspoons peanut oil
2 garlic cloves, minced
1–2 teaspoons soy sauce
1 teaspoon minced ginger
1 fresh green or red chilli, finely chopped
Coriander (cilantro) and lemon wedges, to serve

1. Spray a sheet of foil with oil. Lay the fish on the foil skin-side down in a single layer. Cover with lemon slices and sprinkle with the spring onions.
2. Combine the remaining ingredients. Drizzle half the sauce over the fish. Cover with more foil and fold the edges to seal, making a parcel. Place into the slow cooker.
3. Cover and cook on HIGH for 2 hours, or until flesh flakes when tested with a fork.
4. Serve with coriander, lemon wedges and remaining sauce.

Robyn Clark

Garlic & Herb Fish Bites

A satisfying snack, appetiser, main or side, these fish bites are sure to surprise with their versatility. They have a triple herb infused coating to give your fish that oomph it can sometimes lack.

Serves 4 as a main • Preparation 15 mins • Cook 1 hour • Cooker capacity 7 litres

1 egg
½ cup breadcrumbs
½ teaspoon garlic powder
¼ teaspoon dried oregano
¼ teaspoon dried thyme
¼ teaspoon dried tarragon
400 g (14 oz) barramundi middle fillets (or fish fillets of choice)
Salad, to serve

1. Line the slow cooker with baking paper. Lightly beat the egg in a bowl, and combine the breadcrumbs and herbs in another bowl.
2. Cut the fish into bite-sized pieces or strips. Brush fish pieces individually with egg, then roll in breadcrumb mixture to coat.
3. Place into the slow cooker, leaving a gap between pieces.
4. Cover, putting a tea towel (dish towel) under the lid, and cook on HIGH for 30 minutes. Turn over and cook for a further 30 minutes.
5. Serve with salad.

Simon Christie

Creamy Garlic Prawn Risotto

I absolutely love my risotto, but with two kids running around causing mischief I always forget it's on the stove! By putting it in the slow cooker I can forget about it and still enjoy delicious creamy goodness for dinner.

Serves 4 • Preparation 15 mins • Cook 3 hours • Cooker capacity 5 litres

4 cups chicken stock
1½ cups arborio rice
1 cup grated parmesan cheese, plus extra to serve
1 onion, diced
½ cup white wine
2 garlic cloves, minced
2 cups peeled raw prawns (shrimp)
1 cup baby spinach leaves

1. Combine the stock, rice, parmesan, onion, wine and garlic in the slow cooker.
2. Cover and cook on HIGH for 2 hours.
3. Add the prawns and spinach and cook for a further 1 hour.
4. Season with salt and pepper, and serve with extra parmesan on top.

Emily James

Tuna & Veggie-packed Pasta Bake

This is a great way to hide veggies from the kids. This pasta bake will not only win over the kids but the grown-ups too.

Serves 6 • Preparation 15 mins • Cook 4 hours • Cooker capacity 5.5 litres

½ cup plain (all-purpose) flour
4½ cups milk
350 g (12½ oz) pasta
1 zucchini, grated
1 carrot, grated
1 onion, chopped
4 tablespoons butter
70 g (2 ⅓ oz) broccoli florets, roughly chopped
60 g (2 oz) corn kernels
1 tablespoon vegetable stock concentrate
2 garlic cloves, minced
425 g (15 oz) can tuna, drained and flaked
70 g (2 ⅓ oz) tasty cheese, grated

1. Place the flour into a bowl and gradually add the milk, whisking until smooth.
2. Place the milk mixture and the remaining ingredients except the tuna and cheese in the slow cooker and stir until evenly combined. Season with pepper.
3. Cover and cook on LOW for 2 hours.
4. Add the tuna and cook for 1 hour.
5. Sprinkle with the cheese and cook for a further 1 hour.

Denise Roberts

VEGETARIAN

Dahl Slow Cooker Style

This is something I make for myself in my small cooker. It's a great meat substitute when it's the end of the week before shopping day (and pay day).

Serves 2 • Preparation 15 mins • Cook 3½ hours • Cooker capacity 1.5 Litres

1 cup red lentils
½ teaspoon ground turmeric
Pinch salt
20 g (¾ oz) butter
2 small tomatoes, chopped
1 small onion, diced
2 tablespoons minced garlic
2 teaspoons ground coriander
¾ teaspoon cumin seeds
½-1 teaspoon ground chilli (to your taste)
Squeeze lemon juice and Greek yoghurt, to serve

1. Rinse the lentils in cold water to remove any scum. Place into the slow cooker with the turmeric, salt and 3 cups water.
2. Cover and cook on HIGH for 1 hour.
3. Melt the butter in a frying pan and cook the tomato, onion, garlic and spices until soft. Stir into the lentil mixture.
4. Cook on HIGH for 2½ hours, until the mixture has a soupy texture.
5. Serve with a squeeze of lemon juice and some Greek yoghurt.

NOTE: To make a larger amount, just double the recipe and use a 5–6 litre cooker. Turkish bread is a good scooper for this meal.

Robyn Clark

Baked Sweet Potato Eggs

I admit it – I love sweet potato. When cooked until tender, that sweet flesh just scoops right out. Adding eggs is a great way to take them to the next level for a yummy lunch or dinner.

Serves 2 • Preparation 5 mins • Cook 2 hours • Cooker capacity 5 litres

1 large sweet potato
2 eggs
Salad or grilled mushrooms, to serve (optional)

1. Cut the sweet potato in half lengthways. Place the halves into the slow cooker, cut side up.
2. Cover and cook on HIGH for about 1 hour and 45 minutes or until tender.
3. Carefully take the sweet potato out of the slow cooker. Scoop out enough of the soft flesh to allow room to crack an egg into each hollow. Place the sweet potatoes back into the slow cooker then crack an egg into each. Season with salt and cracked black pepper.
4. Cover and cook for a further 20 minutes, or until the eggs are done to your liking. Serve with a side salad or grilled mushrooms, if you like.

NOTE: I cook the sweet potatoes directly on the base of my non-ceramic slow cooker. If using a ceramic bowl I would elevate them on a trivet over 1–2 cm (about ½ inch) of water.

Paulene Christie

Judy's Chickpea Ragout

This recipe came about after I tasted a similar dish from a buffet. I went home and fiddled to come up with a slow cooker version. I like this recipe because it is flexible, simple and economical. It is always gobbled up, even by my meat lovers. It can be served as a side to any meat or fish, alone, or with crusty bread, rice or pasta. It can even be used for breakfast in place of baked beans with a poached egg. If you don't have the veggies in the list, replace them with other veggies.

Serves 6–8 • Preparation 15 mins • Cook 7–8 hours • Cooker capacity 6 litres

2 x 400 g (14 oz) cans chickpeas, rinsed and drained
2 cups vegetable stock
400 g (14 oz) can diced tomatoes
1–2 cups cauliflower florets
1 sweet potato, diced
2 carrots, diced
2 celery stalks, diced
1 capsicum (pepper), diced
1 onion, diced
2 tablespoons tomato paste (concentrated puree)
2 garlic cloves, minced
1–2 tsp chilli paste, hot sauce or chopped chilli
Greek yoghurt, chopped chives and parsley, to serve

1. Put all the ingredients into the slow cooker, season with crushed black pepper and mix well.
2. Cover and cook on LOW for 7–8 hours.
3. Serve topped with a dollop of yoghurt and sprinkled with chives and parsley.

NOTE: Don't be afraid to substitute in this recipe. I use vegetables that are in season and cheap on the day. Variations could include potato, zucchini, mushrooms, sweet corn, leek or baby spinach.

Judy Maughan

Tasty Tofu & Capsicum

Some people turn their noses up at tofu, but this recipe is so tasty that even my meat-loving sons enjoy it!

Serves: 6 • Preparation: 10 mins + 15 mins marinating • Cook time 4 hours • Cooker capacity: 6 litres

375 g (13 oz) firm tofu, cut into cubes
⅓ cup kecap manis (sweet soy sauce)
2 x 400 g (14 oz) cans diced tomatoes
1 onion, chopped
2 garlic cloves, minced
1 teaspoon dried Italian herbs
1 large green capsicum (pepper), sliced
Rice and sweet chilli sauce, to serve

1. Mix tofu with kecap manis, coating completely. Leave to marinate for at least 15 minutes, or overnight in the fridge.
2. Place tofu into the slow cooker. Add the tomatoes, onion, garlic and herbs. Stir gently to combine.
3. Cover and cook on HIGH for 3 hours. Add the capsicum and cook for 1 hour.
4. Serve on a bed of rice with a good slug of sweet chilli sauce.

NOTE: Cook on LOW for 8 hours if you prefer.

Fiona Masters

Cheese & Vegetable Frittata

We love this recipe as a fresh summer meal served with salad and coleslaw. The frittata can also be sliced into squares for lunchboxes or your next party.

Serves 8 • Preparation 10 mins • Cook 1½ hours • Cooker capacity 5 litres

10 eggs
1 cup grated cheddar cheese
½ red capsicum (pepper), diced
½ yellow capsicum (pepper), diced
1 tomato, diced
1 small onion, finely diced
3 spring onions (scallions), sliced

1. Whisk the eggs in large bowl, then fold the remaining ingredients through.
2. Line the slow cooker with baking paper, then pour in the egg mixture.
3. Cover, putting a tea towel (dish towel) under the lid, and cook on HIGH for 1½ hours. Cooking times may vary so test that the egg is cooked through. Use the baking paper to lift the frittata up and out.

NOTE: For a non-vegetarian version, add 200 g (7 oz) diced ham steaks to the mixture.

Paulene Christie

Spinach & Ricotta Lasagne

My husband loves spinach and ricotta meals. I have always found ricotta a bit bland so I came up with this recipe to add more flavour to both the ricotta and the tomato sauce mixture. The result was a very tasty lasagne that was also budget friendly.

Serves 6 • Preparation 20 mins • Cook 4 hours • Capacity 6 litres

750 g (1 lb 11 oz) ricotta
500 g (1 lb 2 oz) frozen spinach, thawed and drained
200 g (7 oz) Danish feta cheese (or any creamy feta), crumbled
½ cup grated parmesan cheese
2 eggs, lightly beaten
Chopped parsley, to taste
700 g (1 lb 9 oz) bottle passata (pureed tomato)
1 tablespoon dried onion flakes
1 teaspoon dried garlic granules
3 teaspoons sugar
Fresh or dried herbs, to taste (see note)
250 g (9 oz) dried lasagne sheets
Grated cheese, to sprinkle on top

1. Place the ricotta, spinach, feta, parmesan, eggs and parsley into a bowl. Season with salt and pepper, and mix until combined.
2. Combine the passata, onion, garlic, sugar, herbs and 1 cup water in another bowl. Season with salt and pepper.
3. To assemble, spread a layer of the tomato sauce on the bottom of the slow cooker. Add a layer of lasagne sheets, then a layer of ricotta mixture. Repeat layering, finishing with a layer of tomato sauce. Sprinkle with cheese.
4. Cover and cook on LOW for 4 hours.

NOTE: You can use fresh herbs such as fresh oregano, basil and parsley. You could also use pizza seasoning or Italian seasoning in the sauce.

Ollie Gamble

DESSERTS & SWEETS

Banana Strawberry Chocolate Cake

This is my favourite cake recipe. Use low fat yoghurt (or low fat custard) and wholemeal flour for a healthier version if you like.

Serves 8 • Preparation 20 mins • Cook 2 hours • Cooker capacity 6 litres

1 cup strawberry yoghurt
2 eggs
1 tablespoon honey
1½ cups self-raising flour
1 teaspoon bicarbonate of soda (baking soda)
1 large or 2 small bananas, mashed
1 cup choc chips

1. Line a loaf tin with baking paper. Whisk the yoghurt, eggs and honey together in a mixing bowl. Mix in the dry ingredients then the mashed banana.
2. Sprinkle most of the choc chips over the bottom of the tin, and pour in the cake batter. Sprinkle remaining choc chips on top.
3. Place some egg rings in the cooker then put the loaf tin on top. Cover, with a tea towel under the lid, and cook on HIGH for 2 hours or until set in the middle.
4. Allow to cool in the tin before turning out.

NOTE: If you have a 3 litre slow cooker, you can line it with baking paper and cook the cake straight in the cooker bowl.

Robyn Clark

Apple and Sultana Snack Bites

This is another win for puff pastry in the slow cooker. These sweet, yet somewhat healthy snacks are perfect for lunchboxes or when you're enjoying a coffee or tea with friends.

Makes 18 • Preparation 15 mins • Cook 1½ hours • Cooker capacity 6 litres

1 green apple, cored and cut into 1 cm (½ inch) dice
100 g (3½ oz) sultanas
1 teaspoon ground cinnamon or nutmeg
2 sheets puff pastry
1 egg, lightly beaten
Spray oil

1. Combine the apple, sultanas and cinnamon in a bowl.
2. Cut each sheet of pastry into nine equal squares.
3. Spoon a little of the apple mixture onto each square, dividing evenly. Fold over to enclose filling, and pinch pastry to seal. Brush with beaten egg.
4. Spray the slow cooker bowl lightly with oil or line with baking paper. Place bites into slow cooker.
5. Cover, putting a tea towel (dish towel) under the lid, and cook on HIGH for 1½ hours.

Simon Christie

Spiced Fudge

This is a recipe I found when wanting to make a Christmas-themed fudge that wasn't chocolate based. It works so well in the slow cooker, goes a long way and has an awesome flavour.

Makes approx 144 pieces • Preparation 15 mins • Cook 3½ hours • Cooker capacity 3.5 litres

2 cups white sugar
2 cups brown sugar
½ cup blackstrap molasses
¼ cup glucose syrup
1 cup milk
150 g (5½ oz) butter, diced
2 teaspoons mixed spice
2 teaspoons ground cinnamon
1 teaspoon ground nutmeg
1 teaspoon ground ginger
½ teaspoon salt
1 tablespoon vanilla extract or essence

1. Put all the ingredients except the vanilla extract into the slow cooker and stir to combine.
2. Cover and cook for 3½ hours, lifting the lid occasionally to let steam escape and to stir. The mixture will come to the boil and is ready when it reaches 114°C (237°F) on a candy thermometer.
3. Turn off the slow cooker and sprinkle the vanilla over the surface. Stand for 5–10 minutes.
4. Transfer mixture to a large bowl or leave in the slow cooker if you prefer. Use electric beaters to beat mixture for about 5 minutes, until mixture thickens and starts to set at the sides.
5. Spread into a greased 23 cm (9 inch) square tin and leave to set. Cut into small squares to serve.

Nikki Willis

Peanut Butter Choc Chunk Cookies

There is something about peanut butter and chocolate that makes them so good together, especially in a cookie! With simple ingredients you may already have on hand, these are a breeze to make and a delight to eat.

Makes 20 • Preparation 10 mins • Cook 1 hour • Cooker capacity 7 litres

1 cup caster sugar
1 cup peanut butter (I use crunchy)
1 egg
1 teaspoon vanilla essence
½ cup choc chips

1. Place the sugar, peanut butter, egg and vanilla into a mixing bowl and mix well. Add the choc chips and mix until combined.
2. Line the slow cooker with baking paper. Roll cookie dough into balls about the size of a golf ball. Place into the slow cooker, spaced well apart, and press with a fork to flatten (I cook 8 per batch in my 7 litre rectangular slow cooker).
3. Cover, putting a tea towel (dish towel) under the lid, and cook on HIGH for 1 hour. Repeat with remaining mixture.
4. Enjoy hot, or allow to cool and store in sealed container.

Paulene Christie

Apple Cinnamon Muffins

Imagine a donut dusted in sugary cinnamon, but without the hole. Ha ha! Add a hint of sweet apple and you have our apple cinnamon muffins. They're a huge hit with my kids, who love the sugary topping and the sweetness of the apple. At less than $3.50 a batch to make they won't break the bank either. Great for lunchboxes and after-school treats.

Makes 20 • Preparation 15 mins • Cook 40 mins • Cooker capacity 7 litres

2½ cups self-raising flour
2 cups peeled and finely diced red apple
1 cup milk
⅔ cup caster sugar
2 eggs
50 g (1¾ oz) soft butter
1 teaspoon ground cinnamon
½ teaspoon salt

COATING

½ cup caster sugar
1–2 teaspoons ground cinnamon
2–3 tablespoons butter, melted

1. Combine all the ingredients (except the coating) in a large mixing bowl and mix well. Spoon into silicone cupcake cases, or a muffin tray that will fit in your slow cooker.
2. Sit cases directly in the slow cooker bowl if it is non-ceramic. If it is ceramic place them on a rack over about 1 cm (½ inch) water.
3. Cover, putting a tea towel (dish towel) under the lid, and cook on HIGH for 40 minutes, or until a skewer inserted into the centre of a muffin comes out clean.
4. Transfer cases or tray to a wire rack until just cool enough to handle. Remove muffins from the cases.
5. For the coating, mix the sugar and cinnamon in a small bowl. Dip muffins top-down into butter, allowing excess to drip off. Press into sugar mixture to coat.

Paulene Christie

Coffee Poached Pears

My daughter decided to try poaching pears in coffee after wanting something different for dessert one night and these have become a quick go-to for breakfast, a snack or dessert.

Serves 4 • Preparation 10 mins • Cook 2–3 hours • Cooker capacity 1.5 litres

2 cups freshly brewed black coffee
¼ cup brown sugar
1 vanilla bean, split, or 1 teaspoon vanilla extract
4 pears, peeled, cored and quartered
Yoghurt or ice-cream, to serve

1. Place coffee, sugar and vanilla bean into the slow cooker.
2. Cover and cook on HIGH for 30 minutes.
3. Gently place pear quarters into liquid and cover with a piece of baking paper to ensure they stay covered by liquid.
4. Cover and cook on HIGH for 1½–2½ hours, until pears are tender.
5. Remove vanilla bean from poaching liquid. Serve pears drizzled with some of the syrup, with yoghurt or ice-cream.

NOTE: Pears will keep for 3–4 days in the fridge in a sealed container. They can also be served for breakfast with yoghurt and/or cereal. For a delicious accompaniment, mix 100 g (3½ oz) yoghurt or vanilla ice-cream with 1 tablespoon honey and ¼ teaspoon ground cinnamon.

Felicity Barnett

Caramel Rice Pudding

I got a bit bored with the traditional rice pudding and thought I'd change it a bit. I'm glad I did because this is so good and I can never eat just one serving of it. I love the way it tastes, especially when I pair it with ice-cream and some cream – nothing better than that.

Serves 3–4 • Preparation 5 mins • Cook 2½ hours • Cooker capacity 6 litres

¾ cup long-grain rice
3 cups milk
¾ cup white sugar
½ cup caramel sauce or topping, plus extra to serve
1 teaspoon ground cinnamon
Ice-cream and/or cream, to serve

1. Lightly grease the slow cooker. Rinse the rice and place into the slow cooker. Add the milk, sugar, caramel sauce and cinnamon.
2. Cover and cook on HIGH for 2½ hours, or until the rice has absorbed most of the liquid.
3. Serve topped with extra caramel sauce, and ice-cream and cream.

Trinity Simmons

French Toast Dessert

I was saddened by the tragedy and losses of the terrorist attacks in Paris in 2015. With France on my mind, I came home for work one day and set about making this French dessert to complement the French-inspired main course on page 206. I hope you too will enjoy both. Bon appetit.

Serves 4 • Preparation 10 mins • Cook 40 mins • Cooker capacity 7 litres

2 tablespoons unsalted butter
4 large egg yolks
1 cup double cream
¼ cup caster sugar
2 teaspoons vanilla essence
¼ teaspoon ground cinnamon
4 brioche slices, 2.5cm (1 inch) thick
¼ teaspoon icing sugar
Ice-cream, to serve

1. Pre-heat slow cooker on HIGH, then add butter.
2. Combine the egg yolks, cream, sugar, vanilla and cinnamon in a large shallow dish.
3. Place brioche in the egg mixture, turning to soak both sides.
4. Place into the slow cooker with the lid off and cook on HIGH for 20 minutes. Turn bread gently with egg flip and cook for a further 20 minutes.
5. Serve dusted with icing sugar, with a scoop of ice-cream.

Simon Christie

Choc Ripple Raspberry Gels

These are great for kids' parties or a sneaky treat after dinner. A simple, unique, recipe with a melt-in-your-mouth raspberry hit and a choc crunch.

Makes 32 • Preparation 5 mins • Cook 40 mins • Cooker capacity 1.5 litres

360 g/12½ oz raspberry jelly lollies (candies) (2 packets)
5 chocolate ripple biscuits

1. Put the jellies into the slow cooker.
2. Cook, uncovered, for 40 minutes or until melted, thick and glossy, stirring occasionally.
3. Line a 20 cm (8 inch) square pan with baking paper. Roughly crush 4 of the biscuits and fold into the melted mixture. Using a silicone spatula, scrape into the prepared pan.
4. Finely crush the remaining biscuit and sprinkle over the surface. Press in lightly with the back of a spoon.
5. Place into the fridge for several hours, until set. Cut into bite-sized pieces, and store in a sealed container lined with baking paper.

Simon Christie

Easy Moist Carrot Cake

This recipe is adapted from my favourite banana custard cake. It makes a nice and easy moist carrot cake that everyone loves.

Serves 8 • Preparation 20 mins • Cook 2 hours • Cooker capacity 6 litres

1 cup plain yoghurt
2 eggs
2 tablespoons vegetable oil
1 tablespoon honey
1½ cups wholemeal self-raising flour
1 teaspoon bicarbonate of soda (baking soda)
1 teaspoon ground cinnamon
½ teaspoon ground nutmeg
2 small carrots, finely grated
Handful each chopped walnuts and chopped dates (optional)

1. Line a loaf tin with baking paper. Whisk the yoghurt, eggs, oil and honey together in a mixing bowl, then stir in the dry ingredients.
2. Fold in the carrots, and the walnuts and dates (if using). Place into the prepared tin.
3. Cover, putting a tea towel (dish towel) under the lid, and cook on HIGH for 2 hours or until set in the middle.
4. Allow to cool in the tin before turning out.

NOTE: If you have a 3 litre slow cooker, you can line it with baking paper and cook the cake straight in the cooker bowl. Use white flour if you prefer.

Robyn Clark

Peanut Butter Mug Cake

Could it get any easier than this? Just three ingredients to assemble. Just 30 minutes to cook. Then you too could be tucking into this fluffy, tasty mug cake! You know you want to…

Serves 1 • Preparation 5 mins • Cook 30 mins • Cooker capacity 5 litres

3 tablespoon peanut butter
1 egg
1 tablespoon sugar

1. Whisk all ingredients until well combined. Pour batter into a mug.
2. Pour 1 cm (½ inch) warm water into the slow cooker and gently sit the cup in the water.
3. Cover, putting a tea towel (dish towel) under the lid, and cook on HIGH for 30 minutes.

NOTE: You could multiply the ingredients to make as many mug cakes as you need. One cake fills about half a standard mug.

Paulene Christie

Choc Orange Cookie Pudding

A really simple and easy pudding. It's versatile, as you can swap the oranges for any fruit of your choice.

Serves 4 • Preparation 5 mins • Cook 1½ hours • Cooker capacity 2.5 litres

Spray oil
2 x 400 g (14 oz) cans orange segments in juice
400 g (14 oz) packet chocolate sponge mix
100 g (3½ oz) butter, chopped

1. Spray the slow cooker bowl lightly with oil. Place the fruit and juice in the bottom.
2. Pour the sponge mix over the fruit. Dab the butter over the top of the sponge mix.
3. Cover, with a tea towel under the lid, and cook on HIGH for 1½ hours.

Joanne Pinnock

Butterscotch Sauce

With several family members having a number of different food allergies, finding sauces everyone can eat is often expensive if not impossible. This homemade butterscotch sauce is delicious drizzled over spice cake or pear crumble or as an indulgent topping poured over ice-cream.

Serves 4–6 • Preparation 5 mins • Cook 1½–2 hours • Cooker capacity 1.5 litres

125 ml (4½ fl oz) cream
½ cup brown sugar
25 g (¾ oz) butter

LACTOSE-FREE OPTION

125 ml (4½ fl oz) lactose-free cream
½ cup brown sugar
25 g (¾ oz) lactose/dairy-free butter

DAIRY-FREE OPTION

125 ml (4½ fl oz) coconut cream
½ cup brown sugar
1 teaspoon dairy-free butter

1. Turn slow cooker to LOW. Add the cream, sugar and butter.
2. When the butter has melted, stir gently with a silicone spoon, spatula or whisk to combine the ingredients.
3. Cook, uncovered, on LOW for 1½–2 hours, until it is a dark caramel colour and is becoming thick (it will thicken more on cooling). Stir occasionally to prevent burning as there can be hot patches.
4. Pour into a jug to serve, or store in a jar in the fridge for up to 4 days.

NOTE: Avoid scraping the sides of the slow cooker because the sauce may end up with grainy bits. If this does happen pour through a strainer to remove before serving or storing. The dairy-free version doesn't thicken as much, so I only cook until it is a rich caramel colour.

Felicity Barnett

Vanilla Cinnamon Pears

Tender pears with a subtle hint of vanilla and cinnamon. Stored in the fridge, this is enjoyed by my family for breakfast, lunch, snacks and dessert.

Serves 4 • Preparation 10 mins • Cook 2 hours • Cooker capacity 1.5 litres

4 pears, peeled, cored and quartered
1 teaspoon vanilla extract
½ teaspoon ground cinnamon
Yoghurt, sorbet or ice-cream, to serve

1. Place pears into the slow cooker with vanilla, cinnamon and ¼ cup water.
2. Cover and cook on HIGH for 2 hours, until pears are tender.
3. Serve drizzled with some of the syrup, with yoghurt, sorbet or ice-cream.

NOTE: Pears will keep for 3–4 days in the fridge in a sealed container. They can also be served for breakfast with yoghurt and/or cereal.

Felicity Barnett

Caramel Popcorn Bombs

If you remember the old Lolly Gobble Bliss Bombs, then these are for you: little mouthfuls of caramel-coated popcorn that will have you constantly reaching for more.

Makes 8 cups • Preparation 5 mins • Cook 40 mins • Cooker capacity 7 litres

8 cups popped corn
⅔ cup caster sugar
100 g (3½ oz) butter
2 tablespoons honey
⅓ cup roughly chopped pecans

1. Put the popped corn into a large bowl and set aside.
2. Turn the slow cooker on HIGH. Put the sugar, butter and honey into the slow cooker and leave for 5–10 minutes, stirring occasionally, until the butter has melted and the sugar has dissolved.
3. Cover and cook on HIGH for 30 minutes or until the mixture is a light golden brown caramel. Stir in the pecans then pour the mixture over the popcorn and mix until evenly coated.
4. Place onto a tray lined with baking paper and spread out. Allow to cool completely. Break apart and store in an airtight container.

NOTE: If you are making the popcorn yourself, you'll need ½ cup popping corn.

Simon Christie

Raspberry Ripple Bread & Butter Pudding

An easy dessert that uses up leftover bread. One packet of frozen raspberries will make several puddings.

Serves 4 • Preparation 15 mins • Cook 2 hours • Cooker capacity 1.5 litres

5 slices bread, crusts on
Soft butter, to spread
1 cup frozen raspberries, plus extra to serve
2 tablespoons sugar
1½ cups milk
⅓ cup sugar, extra
1 teaspoon vanilla essence
2 eggs
Cream, custard or ice cream, to serve

1. Spread the bread with butter on one side and cut into triangles. Make a layer of bread on the bottom of the slow cooker, buttered-side down. Scatter with some raspberries and then sprinkle with a little sugar.
2. Continue layering bread, raspberries and sugar until the ingredients are used up.
3. Warm the milk with the extra sugar and the vanilla. Beat the eggs until light and fluffy, add the warmed milk and whisk until combined. Pour over the bread and raspberry layers, making sure they are evenly covered.
4. Cover, with a tea towel under the lid, and cook on HIGH for 1 hour. Reduce to LOW and cook for 1 hour, until set.
5. Serve with cream, custard, or ice cream and a few more raspberries on top.

NOTE: If you want to make this in a 3–5 litre slow cooker, use 10 slices of bread, 2 cups raspberries, 3 eggs and 2 cups milk. Still cook on HIGH for the first hour, then LOW until set.

Robyn Clark

Choc Sultana Muesli Bars

These little beauties are great for school snacks or for those moments of hunger between meals. My children big and small enjoy these so much that they disappear in the blink of an eye.

Makes 16 • Preparation 5 mins • Cook 1 hour 15 mins • Cooker capacity 5 litre

125 g (4½ oz) butter
1½ cups caster sugar
2 tablespoons cocoa powder
3 cups rolled (porridge) oats
½ cup sultanas (golden raisins)
Sprinkles or edible cake decorations (optional)

1. Pre-heat the slow cooker on HIGH. Add the butter and melt, then stir in the sugar and cocoa until combined. Leave for about 10 minutes for the sugar to dissolve.
2. Cover, putting a tea towel (dish towel) under the lid, and cook on HIGH for 1 hour.
3. Add the oats and sultanas and stir to combine. Replace the lid and tea towel and cook for a further 15 minutes.
4. Transfer the mixture to a 32 x 22 x 1 cm (12½ x 8½ x ½ inch) baking tray lined with baking paper. Flatten out evenly, pressing down firmly with back of a spoon to compact tightly in the tray. Add sprinkles (if using) and press lightly onto the surface.
5. Place into the fridge for about 1 hour, to set. Cut into bars to serve.

Simon Christie

Eggnog

Before I made this recipe I'd only ever drunk purchased eggnog, which I now know simply doesn't compare to the real thing. I did my research and decided there was no reason we couldn't slow cook an eggnog for the festive season. I know that this Christmas I'll be making it again for everyone to enjoy. There are so many variations (see page 268) to try too!

Serves 6 • Preparation 10 mins • Cook 1 hour 30 mins • Cooker capacity 5 litres

2⅓ cups full-cream milk
⅓ cup sugar
4 egg yolks
1 cup thickened (whipping) cream
1 teaspoon vanilla extract
Ground nutmeg, to serve

1. Whisk the milk, sugar and egg yolks until well combined. Pour into slow cooker.
2. Cover, but with the lid slightly ajar, and cook on HIGH for 1½–2 hours, stirring every 10 minutes or so. When cooked it will coat the back of a spoon, leaving a track if you run your finger across it. The mixture must not simmer or boil, or you will end up with scrambled eggs.
3. Place a large mixing bowl in the sink and surround it with cold water and a few ice cubes. Pour the eggnog into the bowl, and stir well to cool. Whisk in the cream and vanilla.
4. Refrigerate for 2–4 hours, to chill. Serve in small cups or from a punch bowl, with a sprinkle of nutmeg on top.

NOTE: You can make this in a small slow cooker (even 1.5 litre) though it will take longer to cook. If the egg starts to scramble all is not lost! Strain it through a fine sieve to remove solids. Keep refrigerated and use within 2 days.

GARNISH OPTIONS

You can top the eggnog with a dollop of whipped cream. Replace the nutmeg with ground cinnamon, chocolate flakes or crushed candy canes.

ALCOHOLIC VERSION

For an adults-only version, replace ¼ cup of milk with spirits such as rum, brandy or bourbon.

LOW FAT VERSION

Traditional eggnog does have a high fat content. You could replace the full-cream milk with skim milk and the cream with evaporated skim milk to lower the fat content. I've yet to test this myself, but several sources quote it as an option.

Paulene Christie

Latte Eggnog

Once you've made your regular eggnog you can use that as the base of a latte version. When I first made this I didn't drink coffee, but my husband, who's a coffee lover, couldn't get enough of it! He drank the entire batch in the first day! Now that I have discovered coffee for myself I look forward to making him share the latte eggnog with me.

Serves 10 • Preparation 10 mins • Cook 55 mins • Cooker capacity 5 litres

3 cups eggnog (see page 266, or use purchased eggnog)
2 cups brewed strong black coffee (I made mine double strength)
1 cup full-cream milk
2 tablespoons sugar
Ground nutmeg or cinnamon, and whipped cream (optional), to serve

1. Combine the eggnog, coffee and milk in the slow cooker.
2. Cover and cook on HIGH for 1 hour, stirring occasionally, until piping hot.
3. Spoon into cups and serve sprinkled with nutmeg or cinnamon. You can also add a dollop of whipped cream to the top if you are feeling extra naughty.

NOTE: Use the 'keep warm' function if you slow cooker has it, for easy serving straight from the slow cooker at gatherings and parties.

Paulene Christie

Cheapo Rocky Road

Seeing all the posts about fudge on the Facebook site, I decided to try my favourite treat – rocky road – in the slow cooker. Melting chocolate in the slow cooker is easy, especially once you have the timing worked out for your own particular slow cooker. It is so cheap to make, and you can 'jazz it up' depending on your own tastes and budget by adding your own favourite sweets/candies. We enjoy this recipe because it has just enough crunch and just enough marshmallow.

Makes 15–20 pieces • Preparation: 5 mins • Cook: 35 mins • Cooker capacity 1.5 litres

375 g (13 oz) chocolate
250 g (9 oz) marshmallows
2 cups Coco Pops (Coco Puffs)

1. Break the chocolate into bite-sized pieces and place into the slow cooker.
2. Cook uncovered on HIGH for 30 minutes, until the chocolate has melted.
3. Add the marshmallows and cocoa pops in alternating batches and stir to combine.
4. Spoon into patty pan cases and leave to set (in the fridge if weather is warm). Store in an airtight container.

NOTE: Alternatively, put the marshmallows and cocoa pops (and any other sweets/candies if using) into a lined slice pan. Pour the melted chocolate over the top and stir them together in the pan.

Roslyn Potter

Choc Chip Banana Scrolls with Caramel Sauce

This is a family favourite recipe and a real winter warmer dessert. I created the scrolls just experimenting in the kitchen. My son loves when we make them together and loves digging in when they're ready.

Serves 6–8 • Preparation 15 mins • Cook 1½–2 hours • Cooker capacity 4 litres

100 g (3½ oz) cold unsalted butter
1½ cups self-raising flour
⅓ cup milk
2–3 bananas, mashed
1 cup choc chips
½ cup brown sugar
2 tablespoons golden syrup

1. Cut 80 g (2¾ oz) butter into cubes and rub into flour using your fingertips until it forms a breadcrumb-like consistency. Add milk and mix to make a soft dough.
2. Roll dough out on a floured surface to a rectangle and cover surface with mashed banana. Sprinkle chocolate chips over the banana.
3. Roll dough into a long sausage shape, and cut into 2cm slices.
4. Line the slow cooker with baking paper and place scrolls in close together, flat side down.
5. Place the sugar, golden syrup, remaining butter and ½ cup water in a microwave safe bowl. Microwave for 90 seconds, until butter has melted and sugar has dissolved. Stir until combined.
6. Pour the sauce over the scrolls (don't worry, the sauce will thicken and soak into the scrolls while cooking).
7. Cover, putting a tea towel (dish towel) under the lid, and cook on HIGH for 1½–2 hours, until scrolls have risen and cooked through.

NOTE: These are great with ice-cream.

Ashley Polachek

Banana Fudge

A simple fudge recipe that is a sweet banana delight.

Makes 20 + squares • Preparation 5 mins • Cook 4–6 hours • Cooker capacity 5 litres

500 g (1 lb 2 oz) white chocolate, broken up
395 g (14 oz) can sweetened condensed milk
300 g (10½ oz) banana lollies (candies), roughly chopped
2 teaspoons banana essence
1 teaspoon vanilla essence

1. Place the white chocolate and condensed milk into the slow cooker.
2. Cover and cook on HIGH for 4–6 hours or until completely melted.
3. Add banana lollies, banana essence and vanilla essence and stir to combine.
4. Pour mixture into a 28 x 18cm (11 x 7 inch) slice pan lined with baking paper. Place in fridge until set, then cut into squares to serve.

NOTE: Use essences according to your taste. Add 1 teaspoon at a time and adjust accordingly.

Kassandra Carter

Apple Cobbler Cake

I came up with this after I had seen a berry cobbler and only had apples in the cupboard. I thought that I would experiment and it totally paid off. It's quick and simple to make and there are never any leftovers when I make it.

Serves 4–6 • Preparation 10 mins • Cook 2 hours • Cooker capacity 6.5 litres

800 g (1 lb 12 oz) can pie apples
Sugar, to taste
Ground cinnamon, to taste
340 g (12 oz) packet butter cake mixture
140 g (5 oz) butter, chopped
Cream, ice-cream or custard, to serve

1. Spread apples evenly over the bottom of the slow cooker, making sure there are no gaps.
2. Sprinkle sugar and cinnamon over the apples. Add the cake mixture on top of the apples in an even layer.
3. Sprinkle extra sugar and cinnamon over the cake mixture – this is optional but I find it gives a tasty crust. Dot the butter evenly over the top.
4. Cook on HIGH for 2 hours or until the cake looks moist but is set in the middle.
5. Serve with cream, ice-cream or custard.

NOTE: Use the amount of sugar and cinnamon that suits you – depending on your sweet tooth! This cake is delicious served hot or cold.

Bibi Kay

I Can't Believe It's Chocolate Cobbler

This is a very delicious family recipe passed down to me and my family. It is so good you can never just have one serve – I always go for seconds. I love this dessert so much I make it for my friends when they come for dinner. It's always a winner.

Serves 6–8 • Preparation 10 mins • Cook 3–4 hours • Cooker capacity 6 litres

180 g (6 oz) butter, melted
1½ cups self-raising flour
½ cup milk
2 tablespoons cocoa powder
2 tsp vanilla extract
3 cups sugar
½ cup cocoa powder, extra
2½ cups boiling water
Whipped cream, cream or ice-cream, to serve

1. Pour the melted butter into the bottom of the slow cooker. Combine the milk, vanilla, flour, cocoa powder and 1½ cups of the sugar. Pour mixture over the butter.
2. In a small bowl, mix together the remaining sugar and extra cocoa. Sprinkle over the batter.
3. Gently pour the boiling water over the top, but do not mix.
4. Cook, covered, on HIGH for 3–4 hours, until set.
5. Serve with whipped cream, cream or ice cream

Trinity Simmons

Fudge Spoons

I came up with the idea of these fudge spoons last Christmas. So often after a big festive lunch we don't really feel like a big heavy dessert. I thought the spoons would make a really neat way to serve fudge as a light yet fun dessert option. It was a huge hit! You can make fewer spoons if like – just pour the remaining fudge into a lined tray.

Makes 30 • Preparation 10 mins • Cook 1½ hours • Cooker capacity 1.5 litres

500 g (1 lb 2 oz) chocolate
1 tablespoon butter
1 tablespoon vanilla essence
395 g (14 oz g) can sweetened condensed milk
Edible cake decorations (found in the baking section of the supermarket)

1. Place all ingredients, except the decorations, into the slow cooker.
2. Cook on LOW with the lid off for 1½ hours, stirring every 15 minutes or so with a non-wooden spoon.
3. Scoop fudge mixture onto spoons to fill. Top with cake decorations, pressing slightly to fix them in place. Place onto a tray.
4. Place the tray of spoons in the fridge until set, and keep refrigerated until serving.

NOTE: I purchased a large stack of inexpensive spoons for this and I bent each one just slightly so that it would sit on a tray without rolling over – this makes filling them easier.

Paulene Christie

Soft-top Salted Caramel Fudge

I've always loved chocolate fudge and wanted to come up with a version all of my own that everyone in my family would love. I knew that everyone in my family loves chocolate and caramel so I decided to combine them. My mum helped me with the idea to salt the caramel and together we came up with a soft-top salted caramel fudge! Have an adult help you to safely make the caramel, then the rest you can easily do yourself with supervision.

Makes 50 pieces • Preparation 20 mins • Cook 7½ hours • Cooker capacity 1.5 litres

SALTED CARAMEL TOPPING

395 g (14 oz) can sweetened condensed milk (see note)
¾–1 teaspoon crushed sea salt

FUDGE

500 g (1 lb 2 oz) chocolate
1 tablespoon butter
1 tablespoon vanilla essence
395 g (14 oz) can sweetened condensed milk

1. To make the salted caramel topping, place the whole unopened can of condensed milk in the slow cooker. Cover it completely with water. It should be 2.5 cm (1 inch) over the top of the can at all times during cooking (very important).
2. Cover and cook on HIGH for 6 hours. Lift the can out of the slow cooker and cool completely before opening (very important). When cool, scoop out into a bowl and mix in ½ teaspoon of the salt. Taste and add a little more salt if you like.
3. For the fudge, place all the ingredients into the slow cooker.
4. Cook on LOW with the lid off for 1½ hours, stirring every 15 minutes or so with a non-wooden spoon.
5. Line a 20 cm (8 inch) square pan with baking paper. Pour in the fudge, and refrigerate until set.
6. To assemble, pour the salted caramel over top of the fudge, and sprinkle with the remaining ¼ teaspoon salt. Return to fridge for an hour just to ensure it's well chilled before cutting

NOTE: The caramel top will remain soft, not set like the fudge. Store the pieces in single layer to avoid smearing the caramel. Keep in the fridge until serving.

You could use a can of Caramel Top'n'Fill instead of cooking the can of condensed milk – but it's not as nice as the real thing.

Caleb Christie

Choc Caramel Movie Snax

These I came up with as a devilish idea for a snack with my children during a family movie night. They were light and tasty and always go down a treat.

Makes 6 cups • Preparation 10 mins • Cook 1 hour • Cooker capacity 1.5 litres

1¼ cups sweetened condensed milk
5 fun-sized Milky Way bars
80 g (2 ¾ oz) butter
5 cups low-sugar Cheerios cereal
¾ cup icing sugar
1½ tablespoons cocoa powder

1. Pour the condensed milk into the slow cooker. Cook on HIGH with the lid off for 45 minutes, stirring occasionally.
2. Add the Milky Way bars and butter. Turn cooker to LOW and leave for about 15 minutes, stirring occasionally until melted.
3. Put the cereal into a large bowl. Pour the melted mixture over the cereal and stir until completely coated.
4. Transfer to a plastic bag with the icing sugar and cocoa powder. Twist the top of the bag and shake to coat.
5. Pour onto a baking tray lined with baking paper and leave to cool and set. Break into clumps and store in an airtight container.

Simon Christie

Spice Cake

This allergy-friendly spice cake is egg, gluten, lactose, nut and soy-free. It also works using regular flour and milk, or your usual milk alternative if you need to be dairy-free. It can also be enjoyed served warm with butterscotch sauce (see page 261) and ice-cream (for those who can have it!).

Serves 12 • Preparation 15 mins • Cook 2½ hours • Cooker capacity 5.5 or 7 litres

500 g (1 lb 2 oz) gluten-free plain (all-purpose) flour
250 g (9 oz) coconut sugar or brown sugar
2 tablespoons ground cinnamon
3 teaspoons ground cardamom
2 teaspoons bicarbonate of soda (baking soda)
¼ teaspoons ground cloves
200 ml (7 fl oz) lactose-free milk
250 g (9 oz) honey
40 g (1½ oz) butter, melted
Extra sugar, for sprinkling (optional)

1. Mix all the dry ingredients together in a bowl and make a well in the centre.
2. Heat the milk until warm and mix with the honey. Add to the dry ingredients and stir until evenly combined.
3. Grease a non-stick loaf tin with butter (or line with baking paper) and sprinkle with sugar (if using). Pour the mixture into the tin.
4. Place 2 egg rings into the slow cooker and add about 2.5 cm (1 inch) water. Sit the loaf tin on the egg rings.
5. Cover and cook on HIGH for 2–2½ hours, until a skewer inserted into the centre comes out clean.
6. Leave cake in the tin for 20 minutes then turn out onto a wire rack to cool completely.

Felicity Barnett

Tim Tam Rocky Road

I love rocky road and decided I wanted to add something else to it one day. I had some Tim Tams in the cupboard and OMG – turned out to be amazing! The best thing about rocky road is you can pick and choose what you want to put in, and the possibilities are endless.

Makes 10–30 pieces (depends on sizes you cut) • Preparation 10 mins • Cook 30 mins • Cooker capacity 6 litres

3 x 200 g (7 oz) blocks milk chocolate
280 g (10 oz) packet marshmallows
200 g (7 oz) packet Tim Tams
190 g (6½ oz) packet red frogs
Handful chopped peanuts (optional)

1. Place chocolate into the slow cooker on HIGH and heat, uncovered and stirring occasionally, until melted. If you preheat the slow cooker first it will take about 20 minutes.
2. Cut the marshmallows in half and roughly chop the Tim Tams and frogs.
3. Turn off the slow cooker and stir in the remaining ingredients until combined.
4. Pour into a 28 x 18 cm (11 x 7 inch) slice pan lined with baking paper. Place in fridge until set, then cut into squares to serve.

NOTE: For readers outside Australia – Tim Tams are chocolate biscuits with a chocolate filling, covered in a thin layer of chocolate. Any good chocolate biscuit will do. You can replace the red frogs with Turkish delight, glacé cherries or any soft raspberry lollies (candies).

Nicole Hansen

Chocolate Zucchini Cake

I was fascinated by the concept of using hidden vegetables in a cake. I was happy with the outcome of this recipe and I assure you that you cannot taste the zucchini at all. This cake is absolutely massive so it works out to be great value, and because it's full of vegetable we can fool ourselves it's not too bad for us. After all, we all need another reason to eat cake – right?

Serves 20 • Preparation 15 mins • Cook 1 hour 50 mins • Cooker capacity 6 litres

1 cup brown sugar
¾ cup caster sugar
125 g (4½ oz) soft butter
2⅓ cups self-raising flour
3 eggs, lightly beaten
¼ cup dark cocoa powder
1 teaspoon ground cinnamon
1 teaspoon vanilla extract
¼ teaspoon salt
3 cups grated zucchini
1 cup choc chips
½ cup Greek yoghurt
Spray oil

1. Use a wooden spoon to beat the sugars and butter together until creamy. Add the flour and eggs, stirring to combine well.
2. Add the cocoa, cinnamon, vanilla and salt. Stir to combine, then mix in the zucchini, choc chips and yoghurt. Stir until combined.
3. Spray the slow cooker lightly with oil and line the base and sides with baking paper. Pour the batter into the slow cooker.
4. Cover, putting a tea towel (dish towel) under the lid, and cook on HIGH for 1 hour 50 minutes.

NOTE: Ice the cake if you desire but I didn't feel it needed it, as it was delicious without icing.

Paulene Christie

Brownie Bliss Bombs

I often lie awake at night thinking of new ways to do things in my slow cooker. Surely I'm not the only one who does this, right? One particular night I was thinking of how I could take fudge to the next level. Using it as a topper on another base seemed like a great idea and it worked so well! The firm base of the brownie is perfect to hold the fudge, but also to help it slice nicely. The biscuit layer in between can easily be adapted to use whatever biscuits you like best. These are so yummy that when I made them for the first time I quickly delivered them to neighbours, friends and work colleagues so they didn't all end up in my belly – they are that good! I dare you to stop at just one!

Makes 40–50 • Preparation 25 mins • Cook 1½ hours • Cooker capacity 7 litres & 1.5 litres

BROWNIE

2 cups caster sugar
200 g (7 oz) soft butter
1 cup plain (all-purpose) flour
½ cup cocoa powder
4 eggs
1 teaspoon vanilla essence
½ teaspoon baking powder
½ teaspoon salt

FUDGE

500 g (1 lb 2 oz) milk chocolate
1 tablespoon butter
1 tablespoon vanilla essence
395 g (14 oz) can sweetened condensed milk

BISCUIT LAYER

8 Tim Tam biscuits (or any you like), roughly crushed

1. For the brownie, combine all the ingredients in a large mixing bowl and mix well. Line the 7 litre slow cooker with baking paper and pour in the batter.
2. Cover, putting a tea towel (dish towel) under the lid, and cook on HIGH for 1 hour 20 minutes, or until a skewer inserted into the centre comes out clean.
3. To make the fudge, place all the ingredients into the 1.5 litre slow cooker (or make it in the larger one when the brownie is done). Cook on LOW with the lid off for 1½ hours, stirring every 15 minutes or so with a non-wooden spoon.
4. Lay the brownie in a 20 cm (8 inch) square pan, then sprinkle the crushed biscuits over. Pour the fudge over the top and spread out to smooth the surface.
5. Refrigerate for at least 4 hours, or overnight, to set. Cut into squares to serve. Store in the fridge.

NOTE: You can vary this with any biscuits you like. Options include Kingston's, Oreo, Mint Slice, Delta Cream, Choc Ripple …

Paulene Christie

White Crunchie Dream Fudge

We can never have enough fudge variations I say! As a fan of Crunchie chocolate bars I wanted to use these in a fudge, and I decided it would be a nice addition to white fudge. This is so yummy and sweet that you'll only need a small amount to satisfy your sweet tooth – this big batch will last you ages!

Makes about 50 squares • Preparation 10 mins • Cook 1 hour 30 mins
• Cooker capacity 1.5 litres

600 g (1 lb 5 oz) white chocolate (I use Cadbury's Dream)
395 g (14 oz) can sweetened condensed milk
1 tablespoon butter
1 tablespoon vanilla essence
8 fun-sized Crunchie pieces (or 1–2 full-sized Crunchie bars), roughly crushed

1. Place all the ingredients except the Crunchie pieces into the slow cooker.
2. Cook on LOW with the lid off for 1½ hours, stirring every 15 minutes or so with a non-wooden spoon.
3. Line a 20 cm (8 inch) square pan with baking paper. Stir ⅔ of the Crunchie into the fudge mixture.
4. Pour into the lined pan and sprinkle the remaining Crunchie on top, pressing in slightly. Refrigerate overnight to set. Cut into squares and store in the fridge.

Paulene Christie

Finally, something for our four-legged friends ...

Dog Food

I cook this in my older slow cooker in the laundry area so it is not wafting through the house and so no one eats the wrong food! It's much better than commercial or tinned dog food!

Serves 7 meals for 1 border collie • Preparation 5 mins • Cook 5 hours • Cooker capacity 4–6 litres

1 kg of pet mince
500 g home brand frozen mixed vegetables
500 ml home brand chicken, beef or vegetable stock
500 g home brand pasta or rice
Any other old vegetables or bones

1. Put all ingredients into the slow cooker and cook on HIGH for 4 hours then on LOW for 1 hour.

Lol Doyle

INDEX

C

H

K

L

M

Q

R

THANK YOU

Thank you to the incredible team of ladies who help me with the massive job of running the Facebook group every day: Felicity, Nikki, Victoria, Denise, Karen and Rozi. I am forever in your debt for all you do for our members and myself every day. I could not do what I do without you. Thank you xx.

To Brigitta Doyle of ABC books – you are like my fairy godmother in many ways. You appeared unexpectedly in my life and changed it forever. Your vision for the books, your incredible support and encouragement along every step of the way and your guidance through the world of publishing cannot be truly captured in just a few words here. You changed the course of my life. I will be thankful to you forever. I am so lucky you reached out to me on that fateful day! What an inspiring and truly beautiful human being you are. Thank you B xx.

Thank you also to Lachlan McLaine and Matthew Howard at HarperCollins Publishing. You help with any and every question I have along the way on this journey and you make the entire process less daunting. Thank you.

Thank you to all those I call friends in life. You've all watched me as I have negotiated this amazing journey and I feel nothing but support and encouragement from you all. (No matter how endlessly I talk about slow cooking.) How lucky am I to have such a cheer squad. I am blessed with many dear friends in my life and every one of you is amazing in your own way.

For my family, in particular to my sisters Vicki and Debbie and to my father Marty – I hope I continue to make you proud. I believe if Mum was still with us she'd be as proud as punch! That makes me smile through the hardest of times. Thank you xx.

Nothing is as important in this world to me as my family.

I've shared the past 25 years of my life with my soul mate Simon. Together we share our life with our three gorgeous children, raising them by the beach in the town I grew up in – one of the most beautiful places on Earth. Being a mother is by far my greatest achievement in this life. All the accolades and life achievements mean nothing without you all by my side.

To my children – you amaze me. You make me want to be the very best me I can be.

You are all so loving and affectionate, caring and inspiring. You make my heart swell every day with pride in the little people you are and are growing into. I feel so blessed to hear you talk of me with pride – 'that's MY mummy!'. Mummy loves you to the moon and back again, my babies xx.

To my husband Simon ... you are the other half of my soul.

We have shared our life since we were both 17 – 25 years now. I don't remember life without you. There is no me without you. What a life we have shared both together and with our children!

Now we share every twist and turn of this amazing slow cooking journey.

There are no days off from this job for me, no morning where it is not the first thing I do when I wake, no night that I don't check on things as the last thing I do before I sleep, and so many hours in between. EVERY day. Yet you support me, encourage me to keep going, help me through the tough times, cheer me through the high times and hold me up through the tiring times.

I couldn't do this without you. Thank you my groom xx.

And last but definitely not least – I'd like to thank each and every member of our Facebook group and of our website community, and every one of you who have submitted your recipes to this book and to all our books. Without you I wouldn't have this community I love.

My hope is that this book is everything YOU want it to be too: Everything you need to make the most of slow cooking in your life. Everything you need to inspire you to get started, or to keep going.

We are a worldwide family of slow cooking enthusiasts and I hope we continue to spread our love of slow cooking around the world with this book too.

Thank you xx

Paulene Christie

Slow-cooking internet sensation Paulene Christie is a busy working mum with a passion for sharing new and exciting recipes for the slow cooker. She now has more than 480,000 members in her Facebook group, Slow Cooker Recipes 4 Families, and a hugely successful website, Slow Cooker Central. The Facebook page is so popular that Paulene has a team of seven people (including her husband, Simon) to help her administer the thousands of recipes and comments that are posted each day. Paulene lives in Queensland with Simon, their three young children and fourteen slow cookers.

www.slowcookercentral.com
www.facebook.com/groups/SlowCookerRecipes4Families